BYRON L. STAY

A Guide to
Argumentative
Writing

Byron L. Stay, associate dean, Mount St. Mary's College,
Emmitsburg, Maryland

Greenhaven Press, Inc., San Diego, CA 92198-9009

Library of Congress Cataloging-in-Publication Data

Stay, Byron L., 1947–
   A guide to argumentative writing / by Byron L. Stay.
    p. cm.
   Includes bibliographical references and index.
   ISBN 1-56510-294-0 (alk. paper)
   1. English language—Rhetoric. 2. Persuasion (Rhetoric).
I. Title.
PE1431.S73 1996
808'.042—dc20   95-33057
                                                 CIP

Acknowledgements

I would like to thank a number of people who have been instrumental in the development of this text. First, I am grateful to those who have read and commented on the chapters throughout their various drafts: William Buckley, John Drummond, Michael Finnerty, Muriel Harris, Robert Krzywiec, Martin Malone, Christina Murphy, Steve Newmann, Thomas Mullely, and my editors, Bonnie Szumski and Brenda Griffing.

I have also appreciated the response of my argumentative writing classes and the help of Charles Fisher, Don K. Pierstorff, Carmen Schmersahl, and Sarah Sinopoli during the conceptual stage of this project.

I am particularly indebted to my friend Carl Glover, whose many suggestions and good counsel have guided the writing of this book, and Rosilee Litz for her behind-the-scenes work in making sure this project gets to print.

Introduction

The teaching of argument, always important in upper level composition courses, has begun to play a wider role in education as teachers have seen an increasing need to develop students' ability to think critically. Indeed, critical thinking and effective argumentation are inseparable, especially if argumentation is not simply interpreted to mean "persuasion." Argumentation, seen in the more inclusive context of analysis and understanding, implies interpreting the world around us and communicating such interpretations meaningfully. This book has been written to teach students to think critically first, and then to communicate effectively orally and in writing.

The essays from Greenhaven Press's *Opposing Viewpoints Series* included in this text, those used as brief illustrations within chapters, as well as at the end of the book, provide multiple occasions for analysis. Not only do they illustrate argumentative strategies and provide practice in analysis, but their focus on contemporary social issues makes them particularly appropriate for discussions of complex arguments. They can serve either as bases for student arguments on particular topics or as more generic models to be used in the development of arguments on other topics. They work well both by themselves and in conjunction with other opposing viewpoints anthologies. Reading them after studying the related chapter will offer students a rich understanding of the nature of argument.

Stasis theory is the controlling methodology of this book. I first became interested in stasis through my readings in classical rhetoric; its application to writing arguments did not come into focus until I began working with graduate students writing their MBA theses. I gradually came to see that the methodology the best students use instinctively—identifying problems, defining, categorizing, evaluating them, and proposing courses of action—corresponds to a line of thinking first articulated nearly two thousand years ago. Statis is used in this text not just because it is a way to apply ancient theory to modern contexts but because the stasiatic questions are themselves powerful tools that lie at the heart of argumentation.

This book also includes a number of other useful methods for teaching argument. Specifically, it incorporates discussions of Aristotle's use of the enthymeme and example; Stephen Toulmin's model of data, warrant, and claim; and Carl Rogers's model of communication arising from his work as a clinical psychologist. All these models can be very useful in the teaching of argument, although none provides a definitive structure appropriate for all students on every occasion. My

Table of Contents

experience has shown that all heuristic models have strengths and weaknesses, that some are better for use in certain contexts and at certain points during the course, and that each student will respond to these models differently. Students need the freedom to find the system that works best for them and to find ways of incorporating these systems into their thinking and writing.

1

Purposes of Argument

When people think of argument, they might imagine two disputants exchanging heated words over a political issue, each ignoring what the other is saying, and each trying to score a verbal knockout; or a political debate with participants squaring off against each other, trying to nail down the votes of members of an audience; or two debate teams, trying to score points against each other by raising and refuting issues in an agreed-upon forum. Each of these forms of argument differs from the others in terms of purpose and structure. In each case disputants in part are motivated by a desire to "win" the argument. In the case of the irascible disputants, winning is probably the only objective (although deciding who won won't be independently verifiable). In the case of the political candidates, in the long run, winning means getting elected. In the case of the debate team, participants are less interested in convincing members of the opposing team than in impressing a judge. How often does one hear debaters concede their position in mid-debate because they have been completely won over by the opposing team? This doesn't happen because resolution is not the purpose of debate.

All these forms of argument represent attempts to persuade an audience, although what it means to persuade an audience differs in each of the examples. Strictly speaking, "persuasion" occurs when argument is used to convince an audience of a position not currently held, although the term "argument" is frequently meant to include persuasion. Because persuasion implies moving someone away from a currently held position, it's not surprising that people frequently speak of it in battle metaphors. Persuaders attack, defend, counterattack, and challenge their opponents; they undermine, destroy, and tear apart their opponents' positions. George Lakoff and Mark Johnson, in their book *Metaphors We Live By*, suggest that such military metaphors describe not only how we view persuasion but also how we perceive that persuasion is to be carried out. Persuasion takes place on an intellectual battlefield of victory and defeat. These military metaphors, Lakoff and Johnson believe, are not merely convenient handles but are embedded in "the conceptual system" of our culture (63). Persuasion, like argument in general, tends to be seen as a way to convince others of the correctness of the arguer's position, not as a way to tell right from wrong.

Argument, however, can mean much more than persuasion. It can also be used to analyze issues to promote a clearer understanding of them. The case of the debate team provides a good example: while formal academic debates offer a forum for competition between teams, their larger purpose is to facilitate the analysis of predetermined issues. Unlike political candidates, academic debate teams must be prepared to argue various sides of issues. The purpose of debate is really to explore an issue, not to argue passionately for one's favorite side. Debaters need to be disinterested participants in a discussion, trying on one side and then trying on another.

The model of the debate teams demonstrates the importance of using argument to explore opposing viewpoints and expose multiple sides of issues. Argument is a tool that can be used in committees or in small groups to identify points of agreement as well as conflict. In this case argument becomes an agent of compromise and of action, of problem solving and of decision making. A goal of this book is to reveal how argument can be used to solve problems as well as win disputes.

The History of Argument

Although people have been persuading each other since they began uttering the earliest forms of speech, the recorded history of persuasion is much more recent. Most historians trace the teaching of persuasion in Western culture to Corax of Syracuse and his pupil Tisias. After the dictator of Syracuse, Thrasybulus, was overthrown in 466 B.C., the citizens were eager to regain lands that had been unjustly taken from them. In response to the need for a mechanism for legally achieving this goal, Corax began teaching the public, for a fee, how to present claims before a tribunal. Corax attracted a student, Tisias, who learned the art of persuasion well. According to legend, Tisias refused to pay Corax for his services and was taken to court. Tisias mounted his own defense, arguing that he shouldn't have to pay Corax regardless of whether he won or lost the case. Should he win, the court would prevent Corax from collecting, and should he lose, it would be clear that the instruction for which Corax sought payment was worth nothing. Corax, in turn, argued that Tisias should pay whether he won or lost. If Tisias lost the case, the court would make him pay, and if he won, it would prove the value of the lessons. The court, so the story goes, postponed judgment indefinitely (Murphy 6–7).

Aristotle's Rhetoric

Aristotle (384–322 B.C.), a student of Plato's, developed one of the earliest recorded systems of persuasion. Although he left no formal writing, scholars have been able to reconstruct his teachings from lecture notes (his own and those of his students).

In his *Rhetoric* Aristotle identifies two central means of persuasion: the *enthymeme* and the *example*. The enthymeme is a kind of *syllogism*, which is a three-part argument comprising a major premise, minor premise, and conclusion. The most famous syllogism is:

All men are mortal.	(major premise)
Socrates is a man.	(minor premise)
Socrates is mortal.	(conclusion)

The major premise is usually a generalization, the primary assumption of an argument. The minor premise supports the major premise and becomes the subject of the conclusion. Minor premises may also refer to a part of a larger class of things and present conclusions that distinguish part from the whole:

Violent criminals should be executed.
Jack the Ripper was a violent criminal.
Jack the Ripper should have been executed.

The conclusion is considered valid if both the major and minor premises are true.

In the enthymeme, one of these three statements is omitted. Consider the following syllogism:

Publicizing state secrets jeopardizes U.S. security.	(major premise)
The American media have consistently publicized state secrets.	(minor premise)
The American media jeopardizes U.S. security.	(conclusion)

This syllogism could be turned into an enthymeme by collapsing the major premise into a truncated form ("The American media jeopardizes U.S. security because they publicize state secrets."). An enthymeme could also be developed by omitting the minor premise ("The American media jeopardizes U.S. security by publicizing state secrets.") or by omitting the conclusion ("Publicizing state secrets jeopardizes U.S. security, and the American media have consistently publicized state secrets."). The omission of one of the assertions is important because the writer or speaker (the *rhetor*) presumes that the audience is in full accord with the missing assumption. In each case the rhetor must believe that the audience will understand and accept what is missing.

In practice, premises are often omitted from arguments because both the rhetor and the audience accept their validity. Most people, for instance, would accept the enthymeme "Socrates is mortal because he is a man." Such an enthymeme, like the syllogism, depends on probability for its effectiveness. The strength of the conclusion will depend on the degree of certitude the audience has in the premises. For the enthymeme to be accepted, an audience must believe that the major premise is probable—that, in fact, all men *are* mortal, or that the publicizing of state secrets actually does jeopardize U.S. security. Aristotle referred to the enthymeme as a "rhetorical syllogism" because he recognized that not all audiences have the training or the patience to wade through long, elaborate chains of reasoning. It is also possible to construct a series of independent arguments for the same conclusion. For instance, an ancient Greek might have asserted that Socrates was mortal because he was a man, because he was not a god, because his human body was decaying, and because no means existed for keeping mortals alive indefinitely. Each of these assertions would have required its own enthymeme even though the same conclusion would have been reached in all cases.

Exercise 1

What are the hidden premises of the following enthymemes?
1. Destroying wetlands threatens health because it contaminates drinking water.
2. Labeling rock music on the basis of content of lyrics is unconstitutional because it violates free speech.
3. Violent rock lyrics are unjustifiable because they harm the young.

Aristotle also identified the *example* as an important component of arguments. Like enthymemes, examples depend on probability for their effectiveness, although each rhetorical device implies a different kind of probability. In the example, the audience must recognize that one story or experience probably parallels another. A rhetor might argue, for instance, that because unwise investment practices threatened the solvency of city A, similar investment practices will threaten the solvency of city B. The audience must be willing to accept the probability of the example. The example does not move the audience from general to particular or from particular to general. Rather, the example displays parallel phenomena; it convinces the audience by arguing like to like. Sometimes, the examples may be fictive. This example appeared in Will Manley's argument in favor of library censorship:

> In our society there really are no serious and effective censors left to condemn. In a sense, it's kind of like a football game where the champions of intellectual freedom are beating the forces of censorship 78 to 9 and they are not letting up. They're still passing on first down and they refuse to send in the second-stringers. What remains to be conquered? What is there left to talk about?   (122–23)

At other times examples provide stories of real events. Peter Scales begins his argument against library censorship this way:

> In 1986, we in Anchorage, Alaska, noted the passing of an important anniversary—one most of us would rather not brag about. It was ten years since the Anchorage School Board bowed to a group called People for Better Education and voted four-to-three to ban the American Heritage Dictionary. Among the words deemed offensive were "tail," "ball," "nut," "ass," and "bed." More recently, we had a flap in Fairbanks over a book on homosexuality that reminded us that censorship can happen even on "the last Frontier."   (127)

Sometimes examples will work when other means will not because examples make immediate connections between rhetor and audience. Examples, if they are clearly and accurately developed, can be powerful tools of the persuader, in part because they are not easily refuted.

Exercise 2

What examples could be used to argue the following assertions?

1. Acid rain poses serious problems for Maine lakes.
2. Prison sentences for people who commit violent crimes should be mandatory.

Stasis as a System of Argument

As early as the second century B.C., Greek thinkers, led by a teacher named Hermagoras, were codifying a system of argument designed both to assist in arguing before courts and in the analysis of the nature of issues. This system was called "stasis." It refers to a sequence of questions to be asked in order to determine how best to argue a position. By the second century A.D. these questions were placed in hierarchical order by Hermogenes of Tarsus.

In essence, there are four questions of stasis:

> Is it?
> What is it?
> What qualities does it have?
> What should be done about it?

Asked in order, these simple-sounding questions provide a mechanism to analyze issues and to determine the best way to argue them. Only if the first question can be answered satisfactorily does one proceed to the second question. When a point arises in the deliberation at which a question cannot be answered definitively, that point becomes the "stasis," or the resting point in an argument. Stasis is the negotiated place between self and audience (or between antagonists), to begin arguing. Here is how stasis works in practice.

Let's assume that you are the defense attorney for Ernie, who has been accused of stealing a pocket watch from a jeweler. In preparing for the trial, you must ask the following questions sequentially:

Is it?

- Does a problem exist? In legal contexts, has an event taken place that could be construed as a crime? You might be able to argue that no theft occurred at all. If there was no theft, there was no crime, and therefore your client, Ernie, is clearly innocent. The police officer in charge of the investigation, however, testifies that Ernie had the watch in his possession when he was apprehended, and so you must move on to the next level of stasis.

What is it?

- Once the fact of the crime has been established, the category of the crime can be explored. Here you may want to argue that it was not exactly theft, per se. Ernie simply made a "mistake." He meant to put his own watch in his pocket, but got distracted and took the jeweler's by accident. Or you might want to argue that Ernie was framed. The jeweler himself (perhaps because of long-standing personal conflicts with Ernie) may have put the watch in your client's pocket. When the jeweler provides a videotape of the transaction, clearly showing Ernie look around furtively, then sneak the watch from the counter into his pocket, this persuasive strategy has been denied, and you must move on to the third question of stasis.

What qualities does it have?

- Are there particular qualities in Ernie's background, emotional state, financial condition, or genetic makeup that would affect the way the case is viewed? Is Ernie mentally incompetent? Is he an alcoholic? Did he steal the watch to help support his infirm mother? Did he commit the crime spontaneously, or was it carefully planned? In asking questions about quality, you will examine all the individual causes and effects that could conceivably have shaped a reasonable interpretation of Ernie's action, including events that occurred years ago (e.g., perhaps Ernie received a head injury as a child).

What should be done about it?

- Only after the first three questions have been resolved can you move on to the critical last question: What should the sentence be? Should the judge have mercy or be unforgiving?

We can see evidence of this kind of reasoning in nonlegal claims as well. Several years ago when a Korean passenger jet was shot down over Soviet airspace, the Soviets' first response was silence. Nothing had happened. (Question: Is it? Answer: "It isn't.") Only after the flight failed to arrive in Seoul did Soviet leaders concede that, in fact, a plane had gone down, but they insisted that they had had nothing to do with it. (Question: What is it? Answer: "An accident.") When it became increasingly clear that the plane had exploded in air, Soviet authorities admitted that, yes, someone had shot it down, but not them. When information surfaced to indicate that they *had* shot it down, the leaders explained that the action was necessary because the military believed the plane had been on a spy mission. (Question: What qualities does it have? Answer: "It seemed like a counterintelligence operation.") They were forced to move through the questions of stasis only as more and more information became available.

Exercise 3

How might a defense attorney use the questions of stasis to represent these two clients?

1. One who is being tried for embezzling money from an insurance company.
2. One who is being tried for murdering a convenience store clerk in a robbery.

Stasis, however, is more than just a tool for winning arguments. It is both a way to determine the most persuasive direction to take an argument and a helpful tool to understand issues prior to writing about them. The questions of stasis provide a powerful heuristic, or system of analysis, to take issues apart and examine them before making a commitment to a specific persuasive strategy. These two aims support each other. In the case of Ernie and the watch, it is not enough for a defense attorney to decide what position to take. What if the prosecution discovers new evidence between Ernie's arrest and indictment? Being an effective persuader means being an effective analyzer, and that means being able to identify a range of evidence and examine it from the points of view of the audience and the opposition (which may or may not be one and the same).

The Toulmin and Rogers Models of Argument

Two scholars who have been influential in shaping the ways we think about argument are Stephen Toulmin and Carl Rogers. Toulmin's model of argument requires developing a clearly articulated claim with appropriate support. It also requires an examination of the proposed evidence to make sure it is of a kind appropriate for the particular argument. The Toulmin model relies on a careful examination of the thesis in light of the support being used and in light of the writer's often unspoken initial assumptions.

Carl Rogers's model is grounded in clinical psychology. In his work as a counselor Rogers came to see that when people involved in interpersonal disputes describe problems from the other person's point of view before stating their own, they are much more likely to resolve their difficulties. Applied to argument, this means that real persuasion may begin only when the advocate makes a convincing case that he or she understands the audience's position. Rogers taught that the arguer must come to terms with audience expectations, beliefs, and assumptions. He emphasized that before one can effectively be persuasive, one must understand the issue through the audience's eyes.

These two purposes of argument, to persuade and to analyze, reflect the two ways to use argument. To learn how to bring someone to a point of view, how to articulate, support, and promote a position, one must be able to analyze issues, and argument can be an important tool to learn how to accomplish this.

The Rhetorical Context of Argument

Evaluating Arguments

One common misconception about argument is that its effectiveness lies solely in the quality of its logic and support. For example, using terms such as "airtight case" or speaking of "locked up" arguments implies that the issue at hand is completely resolved. However, because arguments take place in the realms of personal interaction *and* logic, no argument is ever completely closed to reexamination. Those that seem to be decided—say, Galileo's claim that the earth moves around the sun—have ceased to be arguments. They have become accepted as facts (as much as anything can be called a "fact"). All arguments exist in a context of writer (or speaker), audience, and message. No argument can exist when any one of these three is missing (unless you like to argue with yourself or rant at a friend). The interaction of these is frequently represented by the rhetorical triangle:

Writer

Audience   Message

Persuaders who act as though the message is everything end up convincing no one regardless of the strength of their logic.

As an example, imagine a presentation on financial investment strategy offered to college seniors. The room that has been rented for the occasion is on the second floor of a dingy building in a bad section of town. The presenter is shabbily dressed and huddled in a corner with several associates who ignore the audience. When the speaker begins, his grammar is weak and his presentation disorganized. He frequently belittles the audience with phrases like "when I was a 'little person' like many of you." In short, the speaker has almost forced the audience to question his credibility. Are the members of the audience likely to invest? Of course not. And yet, this description has said nothing about the *message*. An audience member's decision not to invest would likely be made on the basis of the setting and the way the speaker presented himself, because his demeanor would seem to be the content of the message.

In addition, the speaker's condescension and aloofness would indicate that he does not take his potential clients seriously. Finally, one might wonder why a financial consultant does not have better clothes or why his firm did not rent a better meeting place. An audience member might naturally make many connections between the context and the message. In fact, this audience might be swayed far more by the speaker's apparent disregard for them than by his message. Writers of arguments need to be acutely aware of this potential for dissonance, and they must be very careful to address the expectations and possible objections of the audience.

It might also be assumed that if the speaker were eloquent and had a commanding presence, if the auditorium decor exuded affluence and comfort, the audience would be much more inclined to invest. But would the proposed investment strategy be any more sound? Maybe, maybe not. In fact, a well-dressed speaker in fancy surroundings is the heart of the setup for many an investment scam. People who look and talk as though they were trustworthy may not be any more authentic than con artists who are easier to spot.

This tenuous link between persuader and message underscores the perils of being an audience. How much weight should be given to the *persona*, or "mask," that a writer or speaker creates, and how much to the logic of the argument? How can the listener know whether the persuader is telling the truth? How can the listener determine whether the message is worth listening to? There are no easy answers to these questions. Readers and listeners instinctively sift through information to try to evaluate an argument. The qualifications of the persuader are certainly important. Does the writer rely on personal experience or on the testimony of others? How well prepared and thought out does the argument seem? To what extent is the persuader's point of view different from that of the audience, and does the persuader seem to be aware of this distance (or lack of distance)? These questions illustrate ways to evaluate the quality of an argument by examining the context of the argument.

Such questions also demonstrate how difficult it is to evaluate arguments. The reader or listener who is faced with the arguments of others needs to recognize and appreciate the close connection between message and messenger. Sometimes, as in the case of the investment speaker, the message may be undercut by the messenger's persona. At other times, the persona may overshadow the message. Hitler and Mussolini both possessed dynamic personas that helped sway millions of people to their morally bankrupt causes. Such dynamism need not always be destructive, however. Mother Teresa has a powerful persona that carries her message more than the logic of her argument. She doesn't need to deliver charismatic speeches because her example speaks for itself. Her persona makes the message persuasive.

The evaluation of arguments entails the critical examination of both the quality of the message and the quality of the messenger. This means that the audience has to look carefully at the message as well as the messenger. The messenger may be articulate, but the message is not necessarily cogent; conversely, when the messenger is inarticulate, it's a good idea to look for merit in the message anyway.

Oftentimes, it is rational for the audience to evaluate the message in terms of the messenger's demeanor. A person who seeks a job in public relations by means of a letter of application that contains spelling errors may have demonstrated a lack of care that could carry over into the workplace. Conversely, when a person applying for a job as a graphic designer sends an impeccably written letter and a well-designed résumé, the implied message of competence and care may be accurate. Of course, it always seems easier to make meaningful observations about qualifications when contradictions are found than when the letter and its writer seem to be in perfect harmony. It's better to think carefully about this relationship than to assume that the message is the only important criterion to use in judging an argument.

Producing Arguments in Context

As important as evaluating the relationship of message to messenger is the ability to judge the effectiveness of the message. Obviously, the primary task is to make sure the message is clear, logically consistent, and well supported. Arguments need to be well researched, well reasoned, and well organized. An effective message on investing would have to include accurate and current statistics, a discussion of plausible strategies, and a competent analysis of trends in investment. Speakers who have done their homework will be able to convince listeners that they know what they're talking about.

But there's more to understanding the quality of a message than merely judging the accuracy and thoroughness of the research. Investment counselors do not simply explain why people should invest; they also must be very clear about how the proposed investment strategies will lead to increased savings. A speaker advising students might further state something that not everyone will take as obvious: college seniors should start planning for their financial futures.

To evaluate and anticipate an audience's response effectively, a writer needs to make some initial judgments about recipients of the message: their academic, social, and regional backgrounds; how much they already know about a subject; and their probable positions on the issues. For instance, the poorly prepared investment speaker might have tailored his message to an audience of college seniors. Presumably, few of them will be earning enough in their first job to do much investing. They might, however, be interested in starting to invest on a small scale, or they might be interested in creative ways to pay off their tuition loans. Considering these issues in advance could be very helpful in persuading the college seniors to invest in ways they hadn't considered.

Understanding *Kairos*

A final category might be added to this rhetorical context: *kairos*. *Kairos* is a Greek word meaning "timeliness," or "the opportune moment." Writers of academic arguments do not always have much control over timeliness, but they should be aware that not all arguments are appropriate for all times. Arguing against health care reform to an audience of retirees who fear that their social security payments are about to be reduced will likely not produce the intended results. It would make no more sense for the investment counselor to have invited college freshmen, years away from their first real paycheck, to participate in strategic investment planning. However, auto salespeople know that when they see a customer fall in love with a car, the opportune moment for a sale is at hand. Recognizing the moment at which an audience will be most receptive to persuasion may turn out to be as important as the message itself.

To keep the rhetorical context in mind as arguments are analyzed and written through the next several chapters, it will help to think of the following questions:

1. Who am I? (How do I want to be perceived?)
2. What does my audience think about the issue?
3. Where will my support come from?
4. What does the timing of my argument suggest?

Addressing these questions before writing an argument will help prevent the writer from oversimplifying arguments, directing the right message to the wrong people, or sending the right people the wrong message. Keeping an eye on the context at all times will ensure that the persuader's words will have the best chance of being well received. For now it's important to recognize that arguments don't take place in a vacuum. They occur in an interrelated context of speaker, audience, message, and time. This rhetorical context helps the writer to understand what to argue about, how strongly to argue it, and how to pitch the argument to the right audience.

This text will help you analyze and write arguments and explore the interrelationship between these tasks. You will learn how to evaluate issues, how to evaluate other people's understanding and positions on the issues, how to define your own position clearly, and how to argue it persuasively.

Works Cited

Lakoff, George, and Mark Johnson. *Metaphors We Live By*. Chicago: U of Chicago P, 1980.

Manley, Will. "Facing the Public." *Wilson Library Bulletin* Feb. 1987. Rpt. in *Censorship: Opposing Viewpoints*. San Diego: Greenhaven, 1990. 122–25.

Murphy, James J. "The Origins and Early Development of Rhetoric." *A Synoptic History of Classical Rhetoric*. Ed. James J. Murphy. Davis, CA: Hermagoras, 1983.

Scales, Peter. "Sex, Psychology, and Censorship." *Humanist* July-Aug. 1987. Rpt. in *Censorship: Opposing Viewpoints*. San Diego: Greenhaven, 1990. 127–32.

2

Analyzing
Arguments

When trying to find out why a customer's 1957 Buick won't start, chances are a mechanic will begin by asking questions to determine the category of problem that *might* be the key. Does the engine turn over? What does it sound like when the car is put in gear? Has the car been filled with gas recently? How long has the car been sitting in the garage? All these questions are designed to help the mechanic determine the problem: electric system, fuel system, drive train. In other words, the mechanic solves problems by categorizing them.

More complex problems can be analyzed in the same way—by first categorizing them into the issues they represent. Categorizing problems can make arguments more understandable. When considering issues to analyze and to write about, it is frequently a good idea to think about the *kinds* of issues involved. Writing an argument requires more than simply beginning with a thesis (capital punishment is an abomination of justice; Jimmy Carter is the greatest ex-president of modern times). It also requires understanding what type of argument this is—what it means to be an "abomination of justice" or what constitutes "greatness" among former presidents.

Asking questions about an issue helps the writer decide what claim to argue. Answering these questions will indicate to a writer which stance to take, whether more than one arguable stance should be addressed, or whether the issues themselves are complex enough to defy an easy solution. Analyzing complex issues in order to arrive at a claim to argue requires a kind of "inductive reasoning." It's the kind of process Sherlock Holmes follows when he predicts the height of the culprit from chalk marks on the blackboard (people always write at eye level, he says). Inductive reasoning is used when the arguer cannot be certain of the conclusion because the premises are too large or too complex to be analyzed definitively. Nevertheless, induction is a powerful way to move from analysis to argument.

The need to understand the whole case before deciding on a strategy was recognized by the ancient Romans. Cicero, in *On Oratory and Orators*, introduces a hypothetical lawyer named Antonius to discuss the problem of deciding how to argue a case: Antonius tells of how he comes to decide on a strategy for defending a client. First, he talks extensively to the client. After the client has departed, Antonius puts himself in the shoes of three people: himself, the adversary, and the judge. Only after he has considered the defense from those three perspectives does he decide on a strategy. "And thus I gain this advantage," Antonius says,

> that I consider at one time what I shall say, and say it at another: two things which most speakers, relying upon their genius, do at one and the same time: but certainly those very persons would speak considerably better if they would but resolve to take one time for premeditation, and another for speaking. (II.xxiv.111)

The strategy used by Antonius underscores the need to understand and interact with the audience, and to think through issues from the audience's point of view (as well as the writer's) before committing anything to speech or to print. Although the Greeks and Romans developed systems to use in oral persuasion, their strategies have great use in written communications as well.

There are several advantages to analyzing issues before deciding on a stance. Thinking through issues in advance makes it less likely that an important point will be missed. A writer or speaker who decides on a claim too quickly may fail to see persuasive and strongly held positions that lie in opposition to the chosen claim. One danger of this unbalanced perspective is that the opponent's argument may be seen as wooden rather than dynamic. When this happens, it's more difficult to write persuasively. For instance, an argument in support of nuclear power on the grounds that it is a cheap and safe source of energy isn't likely to convince someone who lives near Yucca Mountain, Nevada, a proposed dump site for nuclear waste. Nuclear plants may be safe when they operate efficiently, but dealing with the radioactive waste they generate presents a troublesome problem. Well-written arguments will address both the advantages and the disadvantages of the respective claims. Only when a writer is able to convince the audience that he or she understands the breadth of given positions will people be convinced of the soundness of the writer's ideas.

Analyzing Written Arguments by Categorizing Them

Identifying and exploring advantages and disadvantages of any given claim can be very difficult, especially in complex arguments. For this reason, writers need to be able to organize the data they are working with. One of the best organizational techniques is *categorizing*. Categorizing provides a way of dealing with complexity because it helps identify all the issues to be considered. Sometimes people talk about looking at "both" sides of an issue, as though there are only two. But complex issues always have more than two sides. Journalists are fond of saying that there is either one side to a story (a devastating tornado has hit the town's airport) or there are five, six, seven sides—there are *never* two sides. In the same way, complex issues have many, many sides, and as writers come to appreciate the complexity of arguments, they become more adept at identifying the points of agreement and disagreement between self and audience.

For instance, John Greenwald, in his article "Time to Choose," makes a number of assertions about the viability of nuclear power as an energy source of the future. Among them are the following.

1. There's potential danger in the greenhouse effect (accelerated by fossil fuels). (55)
2. Licensing of nuclear reactors requires excessive time and cost. (55)
3. Climatological change due to fossil fuel use presents a threat to the environment. (55)
4. Public opposition to new nuclear power plants has cost utilities billions in the past 20 years. (56-57)
5. Some atomic particles are highly toxic. (57)
6. Alternative energy sources (e.g., coal, wind, solar, gas, fusion) are very expensive. (57)
7. Nuclear waste presents a serious storage problem. (57)
8. Yucca Mountain, Nevada, offers a possible site to store nuclear waste. (57)
9. Permanent safe disposal cannot be guaranteed. (58)
10. The cost of gas pipelines would be significant. (58)

All these assertions can be categorized in terms of either cost or ecological consequences. When these ten items are arranged under new headings, it is easy to see that there are three kinds of cost: Those associated with cleaning up nuclear waste, with relying on fossil fuels, and with moving toward alternative sources of energy.

Environmental consequences fall into two classes: those resulting from the use of nuclear power and those resulting from the use of fossil fuels. When reorganized to reflect this breakdown, the points can be outlined as follows.

Ecology:

    Danger from fossil fuels (greenhouse effect)

    • Possible climatological change

    Danger from waste

    • Yucca Mountain

    • Toxicity of nuclear waste

Cost:

    Of current nuclear system

    • Licensing, design

    • Cost of public opposition

    Of fossil fuels

    Of alternatives

Listing and categorizing allows issues that seem to have many different components to be broken down into few components. This will make it much easier to address the components one by one.

Exercise 1

What categories could be used to address the following problems? It might be a good idea to begin by listing individual suggestions separately, then grouping them.

Example: Should college freshmen be allowed to bring cars to Dart College?

Individual concerns:

(a) Freshmen need to learn good study habits (and cars might provide a temptation to do other things).

(b) The parking lots are already full.

(c) Social life for freshmen ought to be centered on campus activities.

Categories of problems:

(a) Academic
(b) Logistical
(c) Social

Now try these:

1. Should children with AIDS be prevented from attending public schools in classes with noninfected children?
2. Should all cigarette ads be banned?
3. Should violent rock lyrics be censored?

To further illustrate the process of analysis through categorization, let's look at the two articles on the use of pesticides included at the end of the book: Laura Weiss's "Pesticides Must Be More Closely Regulated" and Bert L. Bohmont's "Pesticides Need Not Be More Closely Regulated." We'll analyze these materials individually and then examine them together.

Listing the Issues

When reading these two articles, the writer ought continually to ask "What issues are brought out that affect the way one views the problem of pesticides?" At the risk of oversimplifying Weiss's positions, the writer might make notes like the following on the article that argues from an environmentalist perspective.

1. The government is very slow to ban pesticides. (Captan, a chemical pesticide classified by the government as a "probable human carcinogen," is still being used even though it has been under EPA review since 1985.)
2. The long review process for pesticides is mandated by the Federal Insecticide, Fungicide and Rodenticide Act (FIFRA), which places the burden of proof on the EPA rather than on manufacturers.
3. The risks of pesticides include "seeping into groundwater, contaminating food supplies, and accumulating in the tissue of plants, animals, and people. They are capable of causing birth defects, genetic mutations, sterility, and cancer" (68).
4. We may have become overdependent on pesticides.
5. Agricultural advocates like the Farm Bureau "argue that large scale food production is not possible without pesticides and that consumers need these chemicals to control germs, pests, and weeds" (68).

6. Federal registration of pesticides is neither rigorous nor complete.
7. Pesticides pose particular risks to farmworkers.
8. Because it kills birds, the chemical Diazinon has been banned on golf courses but not on food crops.

Grouping the Issues

As it stands, the proposed eight-point list is too unwieldy and chaotic to be of much use. It needs to be made more orderly. Moving to the second question of stasis—What kinds of problems are these?—can help. In this case there are many kinds of problems. For instance, issues concerning EPA and FIFRA reviews appear to be administrative. Those referring to carcinogens, the toxicity of Diazinon, and the risk to farmworkers might be considered "health" issues. The assertion that Americans have become overdependent on pesticides can be considered a "cultural" issue, and the problem of large-scale farm production is certainly an "economic" issue. A preliminary grouping of these categories would look like this:

Administrative issues:
- Government reluctance to ban pesticides (1)
- Long review process (2)
- Inadequacy of federal registration process (6)

Health issues:
- Cancer risk to humans (1,3)
- Pollution of food and water supply (3,8)
- Risk to farmworkers (7)

Environmental issues:
- Seepage into water system (3)
- Toxicity (dangers of Diazinon) (8)

Cultural issues:
- Overdependence on pesticides (4)

Economic issues:
- Pesticides promote large-scale production (5)

Looking at the issue in this way allows the writer to consider problems separately. It also facilitates a consideration of Weiss's weighting of each category. For instance, of the five categories listed, which does this author most emphasize? For Weiss, the weight of the argument seems to rest on administrative, health, and environmental issues. Since she devotes only a few lines to economic and cultural issues, she effectively downplays their importance.

In critiquing Weiss's argument it is useful to ask three questions: "Has this author omitted any categories? What are they? Are the cultural and economic categories more important than Weiss indicates?"

Looking at opposing views is a ready way of comparing the validity of arguments. To do this it will be helpful to look at our other article on the same subject, Bert L. Bohmont's "Pesticides Need Not Be More Closely Regulated." In analyzing Bohmont's argument, one might make the following notes:

1. Most newer compounds are safer to users and to the environment than their predecessors.
2. Pesticides produce economic stability.
3. The world food supply is inadequate.
4. U.S. agriculture already loses one-third of its "potential crop production to various pests" (75).
5. Eliminating modern pest control would cause economic hardship to farmers and consumers.
6. Pesticide use means increased crop yields.
7. The public demands "uncontaminated and unblemished food" (76).
8. The environment can be modified to achieve aesthetic, recreational, and agricultural benefits.
9. Injury and death to some life-forms is an unintended (and unavoidable) consequence.
10. Some pesticides decompose in the food chain; some persist.
11. The public remains concerned about pesticides and has taken some legal action.
12. There is no clear evidence of long-term effects on humans.
13. Pesticides require proper application and storage.
14. The public doesn't understand pesticides.

Notice that many of these separate observations and assertions fit into the categories established for Weiss's argument:

Economic issues:
• Pesticides promote economic stability by increasing yield (2,6)

- Inadequate world food supply (3)
- Crop loss due to pests (4,5)

Health issues:

- Most new pesticides are safer than old ones (1)
- Long-term effect on humans is unclear (12)

Environmental issues:

- Some "environmental modification" is good (8)
- Harm to some life-forms is unavoidable (9)
- Some pesticides decompose in the food chain (10)
- Pesticides require proper application and storage (13)

Cultural issues:

- Public demands unblemished food (7)
- Public concern about pesticides (11)
- Public ignorance of pesticides (14)

Weiss and Bohmont have identified similar issues in considering the problem of pesticides. Weiss addresses the question of administrative red tape, which Bohmont chooses to ignore. She also values health in a way that differs from the way expressed by Bohmont. Clearly, Weiss wants the reader to recognize that the carcinogenicity of captan and the toxicity of Diazinon are reasons enough to be wary of using these chemicals. Bohmont, however, without denying the danger of pesticides, asks for evidence that toxic chemicals are actually used in ways that make the risks unacceptable. He also emphasizes the economic hardship that would result from banning pesticides.

The use of such similar categories by both writers gives us a way of suggesting how these arguments can "talk" to each other. Both Weiss and Bohmont value the same large categories: the environment, the economy, the health of the citizens. They disagree, however, about the relative importance of these categories. In other words, the disagreement between them appears to rest on the third question of stasis: What qualities does it have? What are the relative qualities of the economy, the environment, and the health of citizens that make one category a more important consideration than the others? The writer might also ask whether administrative bureaucracy should be an important consideration.

These two articles also provide a way to begin analyzing the issue. For instance, the categories might be combined in this way:

Health issues:

Risks:

- Cancer risk to humans
- Pollution of food supply
- Risk to farmworkers

Benefits:
- Most new pesticides are safer than old ones
- Long-term effect on humans is unclear

Environmental issues:

Risks:

- Seepage into water system
- Toxicity (dangers of Diazinon)
- Harm to some life-forms is unavoidable

Benefits:
- Decomposition of pesticides in food chain
- Pesticides require proper application and storage
- Some "environmental modification" is good

Cultural issues:
- Public overdependence on pesticides
- Public demand for unblemished food
- Public concern about pesticides
- Public ignorance of pesticides

Economic issues:
- Problems of large-scale production
- Pesticides promote economic stability by increasing yield
- Inadequate world food supply
- Crop loss due to pests

Administrative issues:
- Government reluctance to ban pesticides
- Long review process
- Inadequacy of federal registration process

Categorizing data is one of the more critical steps in analyzing arguments. The step can't be seen as a perfunctory grouping, however. There is frequently more than one possible way to categorize issues. A writer could also identify other categories (e.g., political pressure from farm lobbies or environmental groups). It could be argued that solving the problem of pesticides also involves an issue of genetic mutations. All these factors could lead to new categories, obliging the writer to decide which ones most clearly represent the issue. Some hard decisions must be made concerning where to draw the line separating the categories, and some assertions will likely fall into more than one category. The toxicity of Diazinon, for example, presents both health and environmental problems. The writer's chosen categories must not only be the most effective for the kind of argument to be constructed, they also must be categories the audience would recognize as appropriate. In addressing a town council debating the problem of Japanese beetle infestation, for example, a writer would need to view the issue from a local standpoint, since it has serious implications for the townspeople. Very likely, at least one new category would have to be added: local politics.

By the time the issues of pesticides have been categorized, the first two questions of stasis have been addressed: Is it? and What is it? Answering the first question reveals the existence of not one but many problems. The second question reveals that these problems can be categorized. Before moving on to the third question—What qualities does it have?—the writer needs to be sure that the nature of each category is understood.

Exercise 2

What categories could be used to organize the following assertions?

Assertion: Old-growth forests ought to be preserved in the Pacific Northwest.

1. Less than 10 percent of the forests that once covered the Northwest now remain (Gup 59).
2. Some Douglas firs in the Northwest are 250–1000 years old (National Wildlife 9).
3. Old-growth forests help regulate water levels, which in turn support fish and wildlife and stabilize the soil (Gup 59).
4. The logging industry will be financially hurt without the ability to harvest old-growth forests (Fisher 28).

Assertion: The National Endowment for the Arts (NEA) should be prohibited from using federal money to fund obscene art.

1. The NEA has funded the obscene art of Andrés Serrano.
2. The NEA has funded the homoerotic art of Robert Mapplethorpe.
3. The NEA supports artists who aren't supported in the marketplace.

4. Taxpayers financially support the NEA.

5. The NEA's administration policies don't allow for actively promoting or suppressing particular points of view.

6. The NEA doesn't always receive accurate descriptions about the works to be exhibited in art shows.

7. Taxpayers are offended by federal support of obscenity.

(paraphrased from Jesse Helms's speech, July 26, 1989, on the floor of the Senate in support of an amendment to restrict federal funding for the NEA)

Clarifying Categories

Grouping isolated issues into categories requires the ability to explain clearly what is meant by the categories. Think about what it means to say that the issue of pesticides is essentially one of health. What constitutes an "acceptable health risk"? Is all risk unacceptable? Who will determine risk, and how? We might ask a similar line of questions about the environmental issues. What is the extent of toxic seepage? Do pesticides decompose or do they persist in the food chain? The risks to human health and to the environment in general must be seen in the context of economic issues, as well. Even if pesticides are seen as dangerous, what would be the economic implications of banning them? It might further be asked whether American society would support a healthier environment at the price of economic uncertainty. All these categories must be weighed in the context of all the others.

Exercise 3

Look at the categories identified on the question of pesticides: health related, environmental, cultural, economic, and administrative. Write a one-paragraph definition for each category. Be sure to write complete definitions, taking into consideration all the individual points raised. In the definition of the term "health issues," for instance, be sure to account for the absence of universal agreement on the extent of the risks to health. Similarly, in defining "environmental issues," explain that there are environmental benefits as well as risks. Try as much as possible to describe the whole issue fairly. Be careful not to oversimplify the term, and don't begin to argue a position.

Example: Pesticide use can be seen as an *environmental problem*, because pesticides tend to persist in the environment even after they have served their intended purposes. On the one hand, pesticides may be found in groundwater, in plants, and in animals. Sometimes this contamination can be highly toxic, as in the case of Diazinon. On the other hand, although pesticides certainly threaten some life-forms, not all environmental modification is harmful. Furthermore, it is unclear that the dangers to the environment are as hazardous as some people have claimed, especially if proper application and storage procedures are used. Scientists report that some pesticides decompose rapidly under normal conditions and others may also do so, although more needs to be learned about the decomposition process.

Evaluating Categories

After the categories have been defined, they can be evaluated. This is the third question of stasis: What qualities does it have? Sometimes it might seem that all the categories are equally persuasive. In that case, try analyzing the argument from one perspective and then another. Does one seem to be more persuasive for you, the writer? Explaining a position requires knowing where people place their values.

It is also possible to develop a hierarchy of values. Consider the three categories we have discussed for the issue of pesticides: the environment, the economy, and health. Granted, all three are important, but is one more important than the others? It could be argued, for instance, that economic considerations should supersede health considerations. After all, an inefficient food-producing system (e.g., one that uses no pesticides, and as a result, loses most of its crops to insects) poses severe economic problems that will ultimately undermine a nation's health. Therefore, it makes little sense to argue as though health were the only important issue. One might better argue that the health of a nation's citizens is an important good that can best be fostered in a strong, food-producing economy.

Evaluating categories can also be a useful tool in linking the assumptions of the writer with the assumptions of the audience. Suppose one believed that economic benefits of pesticide use would ultimately promote good health because farmers would be helped to produce an abundance of good, nourishing, and inexpensive food. Suppose also that the audience for such an argument consisted of health care workers concerned about the toxicity of pesticides and the persistence of these substances in the food chain. Since it is unlikely that the audience could be persuaded to abandon their fear of chemicals in the food chain, the thrust of such an argument might be geared instead toward demonstrating to the audience that economic considerations have an important connection to health issues. To this end one could assure the audience of personal concern for the health of the community, making health a common ground between writer and audience. Then it could be argued that regulated pesticide use is desirable *because* of a concern for a nation's health, not in spite of it. By pursuing this line of reasoning, the writer promotes the importance of one category (economy) over another (health) without denying the importance of either one.

Having worked through the first three questions of stasis, the writer can move on to the final question: What should be done about it?

Does the evidence suggest that we should (1) ban all pesticides, (2) limit their use, (3) encourage their use? Perhaps the writer believes that more research should be completed to ensure the availability of sufficient evidence to make a wise decision. Not all arguments end in a proposal—it might simply be argued that pesticides are harmful to aquatic animals or good for food production—but many arguments lead explicitly or implicitly toward a course of action. In some cases the action may be immediate—"Write your congressperson now." Writing the formal proposal is developed more fully in Chapter 8.

Writing Assignment

You have been hired as a consultant to Chelsea Roe, a newly elected county executive in central Pennsylvania. The county has large groves of oak trees, many of which are harvested by a local lumber company. The stands of oak also have recreational value for hikers (the Appalachian Trail snakes through them) and for campers. Furthermore, the hunting and fishing industry provides a significant part of the county's revenue.

However, for the past ten years gypsy moths have become an increasingly pesky problem, and this year biologists forecast an especially heavy infestation. Since the moths attack only oak trees, the county seems particularly vulnerable.

On the one hand, the local population and the lumber company have been applying considerable pressure on the executive to launch a major spraying campaign, even though it will tax the county's budget. On the other hand, the county is home to a large number of environmentalists who are concerned about the effect of spraying on public health and on the quality of the county's lakes and streams.

The debate has been raging for months in the letters to the editor section of the local paper and in public meetings.

The executive has asked you to prepare a report outlining her options and suggesting a course of action. What should you tell her to do? This assignment requires you to spend more time analyzing the issue for the county executive than arguing a position.

Here is one possible way to organize the essay.

1. State the nature of the problem.

    What dangers do the gypsy moths present?
    * How could moths be controlled?
    * What will happen if the oak trees are lost?
    * What public relations problems are involved?

2. What criteria will be involved in solving the problem (e.g., effectiveness, environmental safety, public acceptability of solution)?

3. What possible solutions exist?

4. What solution is best?

5. What are the implications of this solution?

Works Cited

Bohmont, Bert L. from *The Standard Pesticide User's Guide*. Englewood Cliffs, New Jersey: Prentice Hall, 1990. Rpt. in *The Environmental Crisis: Opposing Viewpoints*. San Diego: Greenhaven, 1991. 74-79.

Cicero. *On Oratory and Orators*. Trans. J.S. Watson. Carbondale: Southern Illinois University Press, 1970.

Fisher, Dave and Charlotte Schubert. "Timber Towns in Trouble." *The Progressive* April 1992: 28-29.

Greenwald, John. "Time to Choose." *Time*, April 29, 1991; rpt. *Energy Alternatives: Current Controversies*. San Diego: Greenhaven Press, 1991. 54-60.

Gup, Ted. "Owl vs. Man." *Time* 25 June 1990: 56-62.

Helms, Jesse. Speech given to the U.S. Senate, July 26, 1989; rpt. *Censorship: Opposing Viewpoints*. San Diego: Greenhaven Press, 1990. 36-41.

"The Importance of Old Growth." *National Wildlife* Feb.-March 1988: 9.

Weiss, Laura, "Killer Compounds." *The Public Citizen* January/February 1988. Rpt. in *The Environmental Crisis: Opposing Viewpoints*. San Diego: Greenhaven, 1991. 67-72.

3

Writing Claims and Defining Terms

Claims are the thesis statements of arguments. They are concise assertions describing the focus of the argument and the writer's stance toward it. Because claims need to be clear if the argument is going to be clear, it is important that all critical terms in them be defined. For that reason writing definitions is inseparable from writing claims. Even in a simple claim like "Senator Belltower is an effective leader," the terms "effective" and to a lesser extent "leader" call for careful attention.

In practice, effectively written claims usually are the result of carefully analyzed issues. Let's return briefly to the analysis of pesticides offered in chapter 2. According to the analysis, the problems of pesticide use can be organized in terms of health-related, environmental, cultural, economic, and administrative issues. One way to go about focusing an argument is to see whether one of these categories seems to be most important in addressing the problem. The claim could assert that pesticide use should be seen in terms of the category chosen—for example:

Pesticide use is an economic issue.

Pesticide use is a cultural issue.

Such claims would require that the writer explain not only why pesticide use belongs in the chosen category but also why the other categories don't matter as much. Of course, it's not necessary to write such all-inclusive claims. Claims can be modified in many ways:

Pesticide use should be limited to farm communities.

All government regulations on pesticide use should be dropped unless the chemicals' safety can be assured.

Claims may also compare the relative merits of categories:

The benefits of pesticides outweigh the risks.
The economic issues of pesticides are more important than health-related issues.

Establishing a good claim early in the writing process is critical to any argument. Even though the claim may be modified as more research is completed and more thought given to the subject, the writer needs a clear starting point from which to formulate an argument. Here are some characteristics of a well-conceived, arguable claim:

The claim *can't be self-evident*. Writing that "sports insurance is costly and sometimes hard to obtain" isn't arguable because no one is likely to think otherwise. Claiming that "college athletes ought to pay their own insurance premiums" or that "insurance companies take unnecessary advantage of professional sports franchises," however, could be very arguable in the absence of sufficient supporting evidence, to say nothing of a precise definition of "unnecessary advantage."

The claim needs to be *supportable*. Much of the success of an argument rests on the quality of the support. Asserting that the *Challenger* disaster resulted from congressional stinginess would be difficult to argue because a connection between available funds and the failure of the O-rings (which caused the midair explosion) would be impossible to establish. It might be better to focus instead on causes within NASA itself or associated with the technology used by the space agency.

The claim should be *limited*. Try to avoid making sweeping generalizations:

The United States has historically been an interventionist country.
Computers have revolutionized education.

In the first example a writer would need to consider nearly 350 years of history (assuming that the term "historically" means as far back as the Puritans). Even limiting the focus to the twentieth century would result in a huge topic. Similarly, computers have changed education in so many ways that it would be very difficult to provide sufficiently detailed coverage of all the areas influenced. It would be much better to limit the topic to, for example, the ways the Internet has changed higher education or the ways computer-aided instruction has affected teaching in the elementary grades.

The claim should have a *balanced tone*. A writer who is not intentionally baiting the reader should avoid using loaded language. A "loaded" term carries emotional content that overshadows its denoted meaning. Terms like "politically correct and "enviromaniac" carry emotional charge all by themselves. Avoid using them, especially in the claim. The presence of such emotive words will only cloud the meaning of the argument.

Finally, claims need to be *clearly stated*. This means that they should be focused as narrowly as possible and that all applicable terms in the claim be well defined.

Exercise 1

To what extent are the following claims arguable?
1. Senator Bilgewater's health care plan is the best currently being discussed in Congress.
2. America had more unwed mothers in 1957 than in 1992.
3. Food cooked at home is better than cafeteria food.
4. Ayn Rand's *The Fountainhead* is the best novel ever written.
5. Owners of major league baseball teams are driven only by greed.
6. Convicted felons should be incarcerated.
7. Convicted rapists should always be denied parole.
8. Nuclear energy is the cheapest power source available.
9. Nuclear power generators should be closed down until we find a safe way to store nuclear waste.
10. Outcome-based education is a communist plot to undermine the family.

Exercise 2

Identify two issues that could serve as the basis for an argument. Write two claims for each issue.

Distinguishing Fact from Opinion

Many people mistakenly think that facts are solid "rocks" of rhetorical ammunition and that facts are commonly used for support in arguments. In practice, facts are often slippery assertions that have little force in and of themselves. The effectiveness of facts in an argument depends more on how they are interpreted than on the information itself. Facts are almost never simply strung together for support.

Facts are really assertions that have been accepted as true by a community. Before Galileo asserted that the earth travels around the sun, it was accepted as "fact" that the sun circled the earth. The basics of planetary motion that are now held to be "fact" were not accepted for centuries. Similarly, a scientist who discovers the existence of certain bacteria in a cell may have discovered a fact (the bacteria are there, all right), but determining the cause of the bacteria's presence or its effect on the cell will likely require an act of interpretation.

If you wanted to argue that acid rain is dangerous because it causes permanent harm to the environment, for instance, you might develop an argument by establishing the damage acid rain has caused to lakes and forests. In assessing the damage done to lakes, you might point to the numerous "dead" lakes in the Adirondacks or to the decreasing pH values of many lakes in the northern United States over the past century. Certainly, a precise level of hydrogen ionicity, expressed as a pH value, may be considered factual. Thus pH levels in these lakes, determined by biologists, would likely be accepted by those who think acid rain has caused great harm and by those who believed that the amount of harm has been overstated.

In assessing the damage to trees from acid rain, one could point to a phenomenon that would be considered by most people to be a fact, namely, the decline of the red spruce of northern Appalachia.

However, in determining the *cause* of lower pH levels and the decline of the red spruce, one would have to rely on informed opinion, pointing out, for example, that the National Academy of Sciences has accepted such data as indicating a direct link between acid rain and the decline of lakes and forests. One could say that the academy's studies indicate that because the decline occurred between the late 1950s and mid-1960s, "an interaction between injury from air pollutants and mites seems the likely cause of the spruce decline in the mountain forests of the Northeast" (Silver 102).

The forgoing quotation is not a fact, however. It's the result of very well researched and well documented *opinion*, but it has something less than universal acceptance. One could as easily point to *Trashing the Planet* by Dixy Lee Ray and Lou Guzzo, which takes the same facts (the dropping pH levels and the decline of the red spruce) to be the result of cyclical change. The point is that writers must be very careful in claiming to have "the facts" and equally cautious about attributing the support they use.

Exercise 3

Which of the following statements could be considered fact, and which could be considered opinion?

1. Most acid rain results from naturally decaying organic matter.
2. In 1986 the Census Bureau identified as "poor" a four-person family making $11,203 or less.
3. The fall of the Berlin Wall signaled the end of the Cold War.

4. "Since 1890, work-force involvement by women between the ages of twenty-five and forty-four has soared from 15 percent to 60 percent, with the pace of change tripling after 1950" (Gilder 172).

5. American citizens' participation in politics has declined since 1900.

6. "Voter turnout in the 1988 election reached its lowest ebb in more than half a century" (People for the American Way 101).

7. Environmentalism threatens the American economy.

8. The average physician practices for forty years after receiving a medical degree.

9. "In Canada, as in Britain under socialized medicine, patients are denied care, forced to cope with increasingly antiquated hospitals and equipment, and can die while waiting for treatment" (Wollstein 145).

10. "Studies at the University of Rochester, Texas A&M and Tufts University show that the average cost of developing a new drug rose from $54 million in the 1970s to $125 million in the 1980s, and to $231 million in 1990" (Weidenbaum 214).

The Importance of Defining Key Terms in the Claim

In practice, definitions tend to get very complex. In fact, they can easily become the center of disagreement. Let's look at three different definitions of AZT, a drug used to control the human immunodeficiency virus (HIV), which is generally believed to be a prime cause of AIDS. Try to identify the techniques the authors use to define the term.

1. Retrovir [the Burroughs Wellcome brand name for AZT] is the first and only antiretroviral drug indicated for use in adults and children with HIV infection, and it has been commercially available in the United States since March of 1987. Retrovir is the most extensively studied medication for use against HIV infection in the world, but as a single agent at various stages of infection and in combination with other proven and experimental therapies.

Retrovir slows the progression of HIV infection, allowing asymptomatic infected individuals with impaired immunity (T4 cell count of 500/mm or less) to stay free of symptoms longer and delaying progression to advanced disease for those with early symptoms. In more severely ill patients, it prolongs life and reduces the risk and severity of the opportunistic infections associated with HIV. (from a Burroughs Wellcome press release)

2. Tens of thousands of people are now taking a deadly drug which was approved by the U.S. government on the basis of fraudulent research. That drug is AZT, also known as Retrovir and zidovudine. It is the only federally approved drug for the treatment of "AIDS" (a poorly defined construct now encompassing more than two dozen old diseases).

AZT is not cheap. Treatment for a single patient costs between $8,000 and $12,000 per year, most of which is paid for, directly or indirectly, by taxpayer money. (Lauritsen 166)

3. The rationale of AZT therapy is simple, if not naive: the retro-virus HIV depends on DNA synthesis for multiplication, and AZT terminates DNA synthesis. Thus AZT should stop AIDS, if AIDS were caused by HIV, and if HIV were multiplying during AIDS. Yet there is still no proof for the hypothesis that HIV causes AIDS. Moreover, many studies show that no more than one in 1,000 lymphocytes are ever infected by HIV—even in people dying from AIDS. Since AZT cannot distinguish between an infected and an uninfected cell, 999 uninfected cells must be killed to kill just one HIV-infected cell. This means that AZT, as a treatment for AIDS, has a very high toxicity index. In view of this, there is no rational explanation of how AZT could be beneficial to AIDS patients, even if HIV were proven to cause AIDS. (Duesberg 167)

The first definition, produced by the company that manufactures AZT, begins with a definition by classification: AZT "is the first and only antiretroviral drug" [larger category] "indicated for use in adults and children with HIV infection" [smaller category]. Part of the definition incorporates a history of the drug, giving the year in which it became available and citing but not specifying the length of time researchers have studied it. The release includes a discussion of the effects of the drug on HIV infection (both long and short term). Notice that this passage nests definition within definition. The writers found it necessary to define "impaired immunity" in terms of the number of surface antigens of thymus-derived lymphocytes ("T4 cell count of 500 mm or less") in people who take AZT.

The second passage defines AZT primarily through history (approval process) and effect (what happens to patients who use it). It also addresses the issue of cost and introduces all sorts of new terms that need further definition, including "fraudulent research" and even "AIDS." Notice that the effects described in this definition differ markedly from the effects named in the drug company's press release.

The third passage defines AZT by function (or rationale) and effect. As part of this definition Duesberg provides a partial definition of AIDS as a disease not necessarily caused by HIV. Therefore, even if AZT is effective in fighting HIV, it may not be effective in combating AIDS. The definition also focuses on the adverse effects of AZT, specifically its toxicity.

Identifying and defining the central terms of a claim are critical to writing clear arguments. Consider the claim "AZT is an effective treatment for AIDS." The term *AIDS* might be clearly enough understood with a brief description; *AZT* may take a little more time to flesh out (since not everyone will know what it is); but *effective* will need considerable attention. What does it mean to say that any drug is "effective" in the treatment of AIDS? "Effective" may refer to the success rate in treating the disease, but it might also carry implications that the drug has no severely harmful side effects. If a drug were found to cure half the patients who received it but to shorten the life span of the others, would it be considered "effective"? Clearly, this term will require serious thought before the central question can be answered.

Methods for Defining Terms

There is no single best way to define terms. Indeed, as the following discussion of techniques suggests, the most obvious way—looking words up in a dictionary—often isn't the most helpful.

Defining with a Dictionary

Dictionaries do provide a wealth of useful information. A good dictionary can furnish the etymology (or history) of a word, the pronunciation, the spelling, and variant uses. Dictionaries are especially helpful for terms that have been around for a long time.

Defining by Classification

One good way to write a "dictionary definition" is to use classification as shown in the first definition of AZT cited above. Here is the formula:

A [word to be defined] is a [larger category of things the word belongs to] that [acts in a way that differentiates the term from other items in the large category].

For instance, "A Great Pyrenees is a large, white dog used for guarding sheep in the Pyrenees Mountains." "Great Pyrenees" is the term being defined; "large, white dog" is the broader category; "used for guarding sheep in the Pyrenees Mountains" differentiates this canine breed from other large white dogs. Classification offers a good way to write a clear, single sentence definition.

Exercise 4

Use classification to define the following terms:
1. Box kite
2. Telephone
3. A rose
4. AIDS
5. Pesticide

When you have finished, compare your definition to the one in a dictionary.

Definition by Telling the History

Describing the history of an event is frequently useful in definition. To define AIDS, the writer might both indicate who first identified the disease and tell how it has spread around the world. The definition might also address the history of American public response or the history of response from the medical community. Defining by history is not the same as etymology. The etymology of AZT would include the rationale for the coinage of the parent term (azidothymidine); its history would include the names of early researchers, the date on which it became commercially available, and how much it costs now as opposed to initially.

Defining by Function

Sometimes concepts can be defined by explaining how they work. How does the AIDS virus enter the body? How does it affect the immune system? How does it spread? All these questions address the way the virus functions. The transmission of a car could likewise be explained in terms of the role it plays in the movement of the axle.

Defining Through Cause and Effect

Considering the causes and/or effects of terms is frequently useful in definitions. The writer might explain that AIDS can be transmitted through the blood system (cause) or that Diazinon is a pesticide that when applied to a lawn will kill all insects and any birds that feed on them (effect). As we will see later in this chapter, causes and effects are not necessarily easy to determine. One person might think that AIDS is caused by blood transfusions or sexual contact; someone else might claim that it is the result of loose morals or an act of God. Likewise, while one person might argue that the effect of a national health care plan would be universal coverage, someone else might think first of increased taxes. These causes and effects are not necessarily mutually exclusive, but they do point out some of the obstacles to definition.

Exercise 5

How might one go about writing extended definitions of the following terms? Which of the methods of definition would be most helpful?

1. Cancer
2. Docudrama
3. Field mouse
4. Personal computer
5. Cold War
6. A criminal act

Duesberg's definition of AZT is instructive because it reveals how frequently questions of cause and effect creep into arguments, and especially into definitions. It's hard to imagine defining any medicine without referring to the cause of the disease it is supposed to treat and the effect of the treatment. It would be equally unlikely for anyone to define the Badlands of South Dakota without discussing how this geological feature was formed. Writing about causes presents some unique difficulties, which warrant a separate look.

Chief among these difficulties is the almost universal absence of a single cause or effect for any event. One might argue, for instance, that a crack in the sidewalk caused a rollerblade accident, but couldn't the cause also have been the age of the rollerblades, the exhaustion of the skater, or the unlubricated state of the equipment? Wouldn't it also be possible to place the blame on the skater's sister, who had purchased defective rollerblades as a Christmas present? Even more likely, couldn't the accident have been a result of a combination of some or all of these factors?

The difficulty in assigning causes has been the central point in many, many court cases. One such case is *Palsgraf v. Long Island R.R.*, 248 N.Y. 339, 162 N.E. 99 (1928). A man holding a package of fireworks rushed to catch the commuter train, already in motion. As two railway employees helped him board, one of them accidentally knocked the package out of his hand and onto the tracks, where it exploded. Mrs. Palsgraf was standing at the far end of the platform but was injured when the shock of the explosion caused a heavy set of scales to move unexpectedly from their usual place.

This case raises two central questions concerning cause and responsibility. First, who or what was the primary cause of Mrs. Palsgraf's injuries? Was it the railway, the railway employees, or the man with the fireworks? Was it the manufacturer of the scales, the maker of the fireworks, or even the builder of the platform? Of course, some or all of these can be seen as the primary causal factor.

Once the cause or causes have been determined, the second question can be addressed: To what extent is the causal agent responsible for the injuries to Mrs. Palsgraf? In other words, the court had to decide who or what caused the plaintiff's injuries, who was liable for them, and to what extent this party was responsible for paying the related medical bills.

Mrs. Palsgraf sued the Long Island Railroad for damages, and the case worked its way to the highest court in New York State. She lost. In the majority opinion, Benjamin Cardozo, who later became a justice of the U.S. Supreme Court, wrote that the Long Island Railroad was not liable for damages because the railroad had not created the circumstances that would pose an unreasonable risk of injury. In essence, the court defined proximate cause as "foreseeability of risk." Justice Andrews, however, in writing the minority opinion, argued that the railway should have been held responsible for all harm done in the accident regardless of whether it was foreseeable. Andrews defined "proximate cause" as a continuous and uninterrupted chain of events. Obviously, these two definitions of proximate cause—as a foreseeable chain of events or as an uninterrupted chain of events— can be used to reach mutually exclusive conclusions.

There is a significant difference between remote and proximate (or nearby) causes. It's not surprising that jurists have long debated the definition of the term "proximate." In the case of the scale that fell because of the explosion of some fireworks, there were clearly a number of causes, but on what basis would one decide the nearest—or proximate—cause? It could have been one of the dynamic events happening that day: the man boarding the train or the railway employees' actions. But it is also possible to argue that the real cause was something static that was there all the time—a *condition*. Perhaps the platform was not level or the scales insecurely mounted. We could even become more general and argue that America's reliance on trains or love affair with fireworks was to blame.

Exercise 6

Pick one of the following events and identify as many causes as you can for its occurrence. Then rank the causes from proximate to remote. You might also consider the kinds of cause you have identified (i.e., can you find causes other than proximate and remote?).

1. A recent use of American troops in a foreign country
2. The outcome of most recent presidential election
3. The *Valdez* oil spill

Defining Categories

The need to define categories occurs frequently in academic settings. An English professor who asks whether *Tom Jones* is a comedy or *King Lear* is a tragedy is asking for a categorization. No student would get very far writing a paper on either subject without a clear and probably elaborate definition of "comedy" or "tragedy" (and a dictionary definition will barely squeeze open the door). Similarly, an art professor who asks if a painting is cubist wants both a definition of cubism and a discussion of whether the painting in question fits the definition. These uses of definition in academic settings have been influenced, if not determined, by scholars in the field who themselves draw on definitions handed down from the ancient Greeks and Romans. Using the language of a discipline means understanding how the terms are defined—not just what they mean.

Definitions and causal connections can and do appear in arguments of all kinds. It's common for definitions to serve as support for larger, more complex arguments. The writer needs to be versatile. Definitions may need to be extended into several pages, sometimes into a paragraph, sometimes into a parenthetical phrase; but sometimes they're not necessary at all. It depends on the complexity of the argument and on the knowledge and assumptions of the audience. Good writers develop sensitivity to how much defining a given audience requires to be well informed.

The same can be said for causes. As we have seen, there are many causes for each event, some near and some remote. No single rule will reveal which is the most appropriate cause on which to base a specific argument. Writers should identify as many causes as possible and select from the list those that seem most appropriate for the explanation. They might want to describe the selection process in their arguments, to show that a range of possibilities has been considered.

Learning how to write claims, gaining experience in defining central terms carefully and clearly, and acquiring facility in explaining causal connections are all critical to becoming an effective arguer. These are some of the tools the writer will need to become genuinely persuasive. The following chapters tell how the writer can use these tools in developing a persona and in directing arguments to a particular audience.

Writing Assignment

Write an argument that makes use of the analysis of categories. The categories you choose may be the focus of the argument or a major element. A good way to start is by phrasing claims (or asking questions) that appear to call for a yes or no answer. Of course, these questions will actually require considerable support. For instance, you might consider some of the following statements.

1. There is/is not a world population crisis. (Is there a world population crisis?)
2. There is/is not a world environmental crisis.
3. Condoms do/do not protect against AIDS.
4. Using cloth diapers can/cannot reduce garbage.
5. Recycling is/is not necessary for a clean environment.
6. A liberal arts education is/is not necessary for today's college graduates.
7. Capital punishment is/is not a moral issue.
8. Gun control is/is not a constitutional issue.
9. The president is/is not doing an effective job handling foreign policy.
10. Building a space station is/is not an effective use of our tax dollars.

You may come up with many other such topics on your own. Phrasing questions in this manner will necessitate defining the central terms: "population crisis," "environmental crisis," "protect," "reduce garbage." These terms will need careful definition and development.

Works Cited

Burroughs Wellcome press release. 15 May 1991. Rpt. in *AIDS: Opposing Viewpoints*. San Diego: Greenhaven, 1992. 163.

Gilder, George. "The Myth of the Role Revolution," *Gender Sanity*. Ed. Nicholas Davidson. Lanham, MD: U P of America, 1989. Rpt. in *Social Justice: Opposing Viewpoints*. San Diego: Greenhaven, 1990. 171–78.

Duesberg, Peter. Cited in John Lauritsen, *Poison by Prescription: The AZT Story*. New York: Asklepios, 1990. Rpt. in *AIDS: Opposing Viewpoints*. San Diego: Greenhaven, 1992. 167.

Lauritsen, John. *Poison by Prescription: The AZT Story*. New York: Asklepios, 1990. Rpt. in *AIDS: Opposing Viewpoints*. San Diego: Greenhaven, 1992. 165–70.

People for the American Way. *Democracy's Next Generation: A Study of Youth and Teachers*. Washington, DC, 1989. Rpt. in *Politics in America: Opposing Viewpoints*. San Diego: Greenhaven, 1992. 100–106.

Ray, Dixy Lee with Lou Guzzo. *Trashing the Planet*. Washington, DC: Regnery Gateway, 1990. Rpt. in *Water: Opposing Viewpoints*. San Diego: Greenhaven, 1994. 103–10.

Silver, Cheryl Simon, with Ruth S. DeFries, for the National Academy of Sciences. *One Earth, One Future: Our Changing Global Environment*. Washington, DC: National Academy P, 1991. Rpt. in *Water: Opposing Viewpoints*. San Diego: Greenhaven, 1994. 97–102.

Weidenbaum, Murray. "Are Drug Prices Too High?" *Public Interest* No. 108, Summer 1993: 84–89. Rpt. in *Health Care in America: Opposing Viewpoints*. San Diego: Greenhaven, 1994. 213–17.

Wollstein, Jarret B. "National Health Insurance: A Medical Disaster." *Freeman* Oct. 1992. Rpt. in *Health Care in America: Opposing Viewpoints*. San Diego: Greenhaven, 1994. 142–50.

4

Knowing Yourself

Chapter 1 told of an investment counselor whose presentation had a rather unfortunate effect on his audience. Now we consider this problem from the point of view of the writer or speaker of arguments. Writers of arguments should recognize that they create an image of themselves in the minds of the audience, just as the investment counselor did, however unwittingly. This image may or may not have anything to do with the real writer. It's a persona. Writers of effective arguments realize this and actively work to create a persona readers will trust and believe. It is very difficult to separate the speaker's message from the perception of the speaker as a credible (or non credible) person. All communicators have a personality that comes across in their speaking and writing, and it may turn out to be more important than their words. The communicator may be perceived as angry, sorrowful, sarcastic, or personable (or some combination of these).

All communicators project an ethos—even if all they publish is a shopping list. The kind of language used, whether it is angry or distant, humorous or serious, projects an image that cannot be separated from what is said. An audience looks between words to decide whether a writer is knowledgeable about the subject, whether he or she exudes goodwill or ill will, and whether the voice they perceive is credible.

Starting Points

Here are some questions a speaker would do well to think through before addressing an audience.

Who Are You?

Audiences make certain assessments of the writer as a person that may have little to do with what the person is really like. For example, audiences judge on appearances. When there is a discrepancy between reality and the perceptions nurtured by a public person, the result is a "credibility gap."

Examples of credibility gaps are everywhere. When several lawmakers were found to have accepted bribes in the Abscam scandal of the late 1970s, many voters wondered whether a person who had acted thus was qualified to represent them in Congress. Similarly, presidential candidates who are accused of plagiarism, infidelity, or emotional instability often (but not always) see their political hopes vanish. Credibility gaps may or may not be accurate representations of capability. Many people believe that Senator Edmund Muskie's presidential hopes were dashed when it was reported that he had cried publicly in responding to a question about his wife.

Character is revealed in such things as the tone or level of language, the way the writer treats people and issues, and values the writer holds that seem to be evident in the writing. For example, suppose there has been an explosion in a plant owned by a large chemical corporation. Peter Reynolds, a public relations official, makes this announcement to colleagues: "I am pleased to report that there has been very minimal unfavorable publicity in the local papers concerning the blast. No one was injured." Because of the ordering of this passage, one might be led to conclude that having a minimum of negative publicity is more important to the official than the safety and well-being of employees and the public. Now, this conclusion might not be justified. The writer may have assumed that his colleagues had learned from other sources that no one had been injured, hence had focused his report on the area that represented his personal responsibility. But the audience easily could *perceive* that the wording revealed something about the writer (and perhaps something about the chemical corporation). Audiences always make judgments on who they perceive the writer to be and what the writer has done to warrant belief.

How Much Do You Know?

To be a credible persuader, one must be able to convince readers that all the necessary homework has been done—that the writer has the knowledge to write intelligently about the subject. This qualification can be achieved in part by making sure that all sources are recent and reliable. It makes a difference whether support comes from the *National Review* or the *National Enquirer*. Consider as well whether the support for the position comes through hearsay or serious scholarly research and whether it comes from a narrow or wide range of sources.

How Closely Do You Identify with Your Audience?

No audience wants to be belittled, nor will people listen for long if they feel this way. Think about the last time someone tried to convince you to accept an intellectual position you did not currently hold. Think also about the extent to which the person brought you to understand that he or she understood your point of view. Chances are, the more empathetic the person was to your own standpoint (even if it was ultimately rejected), the more likely you were to change.

An effective persuader knows that the best way to develop identification is by showing the audience members that they are taken seriously and that the writer trusts their judgment. Belittling or talking down to an audience will likely alienate them more than anything else. Knowing just the right level at which to pitch an argument means having to think very carefully about what the audience already knows, what their likely attitudes are, and what their experience probably has been.

You can also consider goodwill, however, in terms of the kind of position you are arguing. It should never be assumed that one position is as good as another or that argument takes place in an ethically neutral universe. Wayne Booth, in *Modern Dogma and the Rhetoric of Assent*, argues that there are bad reasons to change stances as well as good ones. Sometimes, the reader has ethical reasons *not* to change. A German who remained unswayed by Nazi rhetoric, for instance, had perfectly good reasons not to be persuaded regardless of the apparent appeal of the arguments. Another example can be found in Jonathan Swift's satire entitled "A Modest Proposal." The author, who was a clergyman, suggested with tongue in cheek that the economic problems of Ireland could be solved by consuming or exporting Irish babies. Swift's "proposal" is based on a reasonable argument and incorporates lots of reasons for the equitability of his solution, including a demonstration of its economic and social advantages, but they are not "good reasons."

Tools for Arguing

Tone

Emotive words are very powerful in argument, but they can create as many problems as they solve. Consider the following claims as part of an argument opposing the death penalty:

1. The death penalty is not a significant deterrent to crime.
2. The death penalty is state-sanctioned murder.

3. The death penalty represents the tool of the power-hungry elite to exterminate the poor, the downtrodden, and the nonwhite.

These three statements seem to be aimed at different audiences, and they invite different responses. More important, the character of the writer is very different in each case. The first statement is written in fairly neutral terms. The writer seems to maintain emotional distance from the issue. The terms "significant deterrent" and "crime" are not used in a way that will provoke a strong emotional response from the reader.

The use of the word "murder" in the second statement signals to the audience a greater emotional involvement on the part of the writer. This assumption, of course, may be false, but the audience will likely *perceive* an emotional connection. An audience already predisposed against capital punishment may not find the term inappropriate, but an audience not so predisposed may see it as evidence of bias.

The third statement, however, is couched in highly emotive terms: "tool," "power-hungry elite," "exterminate," and "nonwhite." An audience may well assume that the writer has no emotional distance at all from the issue and may wonder whether the writer's clear bias has influenced the judgment that produced the statement itself. Highly emotive words may very well undermine a writer's credibility: can a writer who appears not to see multiple sides of an issue be trusted to represent any side truthfully?

Similarly, strong, emotive words used in argument may or may not persuade the audience. In general, it's a good idea to use the emotions if the audience seems to be supportive but to tone them down if the audience appears to be hostile. Neutral audiences require a little more care. When President George Bush went on national television in January 1991 to announce that he had instructed U.S. forces to start bombing Baghdad, he began by using neutral, factual words to describe in fairly objective terms the events that had led up to his decision:

> Arab leaders sought what became known as an Arab solution, only to conclude that Saddam Hussein was unwilling to leave Kuwait. Others traveled to Baghdad in a variety of efforts to restore peace and justice. Our Secretary of State James Baker held a historic meeting in Geneva only to be totally rebuffed.

Halfway through the speech, however, the president began using more and more emotive terms to engender support for the bombing mission:

Saddam has arrogantly rejected all warnings. Instead, he tried to make this a dispute between Iraq and the United States of America. Well, he failed.

Bush concluded by quoting three soldiers who supported the invasion. The last quotation was presented as follows:

We should all sit up and listen to Jackie Jones, an Army lieutenant, when she says, "If we let [Saddam Hussein] get away with this, who knows what's going to be next?" (A14)

Why did the president move from factual assertions to highly emotive language? Because he was confident that by the time he had finished explaining the facts, he would have built support for his position and could risk involving his audience emotionally in the issue.

Loaded Terms

Words don't just mean a single thing. They carry with them the weight of previous associations. Terms are said to be "loaded" when the emotive content has eclipsed the rational content. In other words, the *connotation*, or association a term carries with it, becomes more important than the *denotation*, the specific meaning one might find in a dictionary. "Communism," for instance, cannot be disassociated (at least among some people in the United States) with erstwhile Cold War tensions and imminent threats to democracy. The term *denotes* a system of government, but it *connotes* a threat. Anyone who uses loaded terms ought to be aware of the potential for language to manipulate meaning.

Exercise 1

Examine the following pairs of terms. What do these terms denote? Do they denote the same thing? What do they connote?

Liberal	Politically correct
Conservative	Right wing
Feminism	Women's rights
Terrorist	Freedom fighter
Computer hacker	Computer enthusiast
Taxpayer	Citizen

A writer who uses emotive terms needs to consider their likely effect on the audience. Probably, for starters, it will be to alienate those who do not already share the writer's stance. Emotive words can also disrupt meaning. Because they carry so much emotional baggage, these terms never mean precisely what they purport to say. Not long ago a candidate for county commissioner in my part of the state ran for office using the slogan "Taxpayers first!" What did he mean? He clearly wasn't just referring to all people who pay taxes, which would cover everyone in the county including the homeless person who pays sales tax on a bar of soap. He meant it (I think) to refer to middle-class people who pay significant taxes on homes and wages. Just the fact that such a term is so difficult to pin down illustrates its fuzziness in arguments.

As an example, consider these two passages on the nature of political correctness:

> I understand the "political correctness" controversy as the surface of a deeper fault line—a trauma in American cultural identity.
>
> America's current identity crisis was precipitated by several events. First, the collapse of the Cold War denied the US an opponent in the tug-of-war between capitalism and communism. When the enemy let go of the rope, the American "team"—constituted to hold the line against tyranny—was dropped on its collective ass. We are now on the prowl for a new enemy, something or someone to mobilize against: Noriega, drugs, Satan, Saddam Hussein or the newest bogey: "political correctness"—a breed of left-wing academic intolerance and exclusion that ends up shackling not only free speech but free-flowing intellectual inquiry—a perversion of a sensible multicultural program of tolerance and inclusion. (Todd Gitlin 80)

> The term "political correctness" seems to have originated in the early part of the century, when it was employed by various species of Marxists to describe and enforce conformity to their preferred ideological positions. Books, films, opinions, even historical events were termed politically correct or politically incorrect depending on whether or not they advanced a particular Marxist view. There is no indication that the revolutionary ideologues and activists of that period spoke of political correctness with any trace of irony or self-mockery. (Dinesh D'Souza 85)

Although these two passages are written from similar points of view on the issue of political correctness, the tone of the arguments differs markedly. Let's see if we can tell why. One of the most striking differences between them is the level of language. Notice that Gitlin makes frequent use of metaphors, from "dropped on its collective ass" to the association of political correctness with popular outrage at drugs, Satanism, and untrustworthy military strongmen. Gitlin writes in the informal way most people talk. D'Souza, on the other hand, uses a somewhat more scholarly approach, exploring the history of the term.

Gitlin also uses metaphors to charge up his writing. He uses a metaphor of play in characterizing the Cold War as a "tug-of-war." He uses geological metaphors (America's fault line of cultural identity), animal metaphors (we're on the prowl), military metaphors (we're mobilizing), and metaphors of imprisonment (the shackling of free speech). All these metaphors, like the loaded language, reflect attempts to persuade the reader through emotive content. But do they work?

Tone is affected even more by the kind of language each writer employs. Gitlin's piece is fully loaded. "Tyranny," "prowl," "bogey," and "left-wing academic intolerance and exclusion" are not neutral terms, and their effect on the passage is to provoke a response from the reader. But do they provoke the response Gitlin intends? The answer may (or may not) depend on your political persuasion. Do you already identify political correctness with "academic intolerance"? Is it effective for Gitlin to do so?

D'Souza, on the other hand, uses fewer of the attention-getting devices favored by Gitlin. His description of political correctness seems less politically charged even though his opposition to the concept may be as strong as Gitlin's. One might be willing to argue that the differences in tone correspond more to the writers' differing assumptions about their audiences than they do to differences in philosophy. Which is the more effectively written argument? What kind(s) of audience would be most likely to be persuaded by each argument?

Not only do these passages reveal different assumptions about audience, but they seem to reveal different levels of ethical and moral commitment to the problem identified. Gitlin clearly feels more ethically committed to attacking PC than does D'Souza—at least his tone leads the reader to that conclusion. Some writers who feels close emotional ties to an issue is less likely to entertain opposing issues and to care about how the audience responds to the message. This is one good reason for writers to avoid writing about emotionally charged issues unless they are aware of the pitfalls and take steps to compensate for them.

Exercise 2

Write two brief definitions of a politically charged issue like gun control, pornography, NRA, NEA, or feminism. Phrase one definition in politically neutral terms and the other in politically charged terms.

There is another reason to be careful of word choice, regardless of whether the audience appears to be on one's side. Using loaded terms to characterize one's opponent (or supporters) makes the writer appear not only arrogant or irrational but overly biased. Even if readers agree with a writer's stance on an issue, they may be put off by his or her lack of respect for the opposition. In all but the most exceptional cases, the best strategy is to take all opponents seriously and use terms describing any opponent and the opposing stance as intellectually legitimate. Remember that Mark Antony undermined Brutus in Shakespeare's play not by attacking him before the crowd at Caesar's funeral but by labeling him an "honorable man."

Mechanical Correctness

Imagine receiving a letter requesting donations for a charitable organization. If the letter were filled with spelling, syntactic, and sentence-level errors, how would you view the writer of the letter? The problems might be attributed to lack of training (or lack of practice in writing). A reader might think that the letter had not been proofread or that the writer didn't care enough about the message to review it, send it through a spell-checker, or have an associate look at it. The point is that *all* these assumptions, whether true or false, present big trouble for donors. Why would anyone donate to an organization that can't control its correspondence?

In the same way, audiences will make judgments about the writer based on the writing quality. Not everyone is a perfect speller (certainly not this writer), and not everyone can write standard prose accurately. All this is beside the point. When you hand in a paper to a professor, put a letter in the mail, or deliver a report to a supervisor, if the writing is not accurate, you're opening the door for judgments to be made about you, your education, and your motivations. People who have difficulty spelling should use the computer's spell-check function, use a dictionary, or consult a friend. The important thing is to get it right.

Formal and Informal Style

It's important in revising written arguments to be constantly aware of voice. Part of the decision to be formal or informal is the writer's. Sometimes a more flowing informal presentation is preferable on formal occasions, which can be static, humorless, and very boring. But to some extent the decision on voice will depend on the context of the argument. Scholarly arguments, for instance, will follow the conventions of the discipline. Perhaps the conventions discourage use of the first person or prohibit use of personal examples. But to a large extent, writers can choose to be less formal even within disciplinary constraints.

Many times people have the mistaken notion that their arguments will carry more weight if they sound highly academic or intellectual. Usually, the opposite happens. Trying to force an overly academic or professional style usually indicates that the writer is uncomfortable with the conventions of a discipline or the conventions of an organization. The result is almost always prose that prevents the reader from closely following the argument.

One of the most infamous memos of the past few decades was written by an engineer in his professional capacity. The quotation that follows is actually a kind of informal proposal, although not every reader would recognize it as such. D. F. Hallman, a manager for the Babcock & Wilcox Company's generation group, wrote a memo in which he suggested

> a change in B&W's philosophy for HPI system use during low-pressure transients. Basically, [the writer's colleagues] recommend leaving the HPI pumps on once HPI has been initiated, until it can be determined that the hot leg temperature is more than 50° F below Tsat for the RCS pressure. Nuclear Service believes this mode can cause the RCS (including the pressurizer) to go solid.   ("Who Says Good Writing Doesn't Pay?")

Before you scoff that this jargon represents the style of engineers, you might be interested in learning that the manager to whom the memo was addressed indicated at the inquest that he didn't think it said anything very important. His failure to understand the proposal hidden in this message (and the failure of the writer to say it clearly) cost Babcock & Wilcox $2.5 billion. What does it say? It says that if something isn't done soon, the reactor at the Three Mile Island nuclear plant is likely to "go solid."

Whatever the writer decides to be the appropriate style and level, it must not be formulaic. It ought to appear natural rather than canned. This will not be easy. As jazz musician Miles Davis once said about trumpet playing, "It's hard to sound like yourself." The same can be said of writing. Learning to develop a personal style requires work and attention to the writing of others.

This doesn't mean that all writing needs to be informal. Writers can judge the level of formality in terms of purpose and audience. Articles written for scholarly journals, for instance, are often condensed, very carefully thought-out pieces that make use of specialized language that may not be immediately accessible to people who haven't been trained in the discipline. This is not necessarily bad, although scholarly writing can be filled with as much or more jargon than non-scholarly writing. Perhaps one of the most difficult writing tasks imaginable is composing a highly complex and detailed analysis within a discipline in clear, jargon-free prose. Success in such undertakings should be the goal of every academic writer.

Exercise 3

Examine the following passages. What observations can you make about the writers of each one? To what extent do you trust their judgment? Why? What observations can you make about the audience that each writer imagines?

1

Most evangelical Christians agree, at least on the surface, that abortion is wrong: few would put themselves entirely in the pro-choice camp by approving abortion-on-demand. But evangelicals still disagree about circumstances under which abortion is deemed justifiable or not justifiable.

If the Christian is to believe abortion is wrong, he should do so for sound biblical reasons. Nothing short of careful biblical analysis will do. Why then does such a variety of opinions exist among those who claim the Bible as their life guide? Not all are sure the Bible really speaks to the abortion question. Some believe the Bible is silent on the issue. Others find a few texts indirectly relevant but not clear enough to decide for or against abortion. When seeking to apply the biblical principles they do find relevant, such as those of the sanctity of human life and the need to act in love, they find the answers to the abortion question elusive.

Granted, the Bible is not a textbook on biology. But I do not think the Bible's stand on the abortion issue is as enigmatic as some might suppose. God's Word is still adequate to respond to the bioethical issues of our day, and especially to abortion.   (Fowler 106)

2

[I] feel abhorrence for the idea of deliberately bringing an unwanted pregnancy to term, delivering forth a helpless human being, and then just giving it away to others to care for. To never again take any responsibility whatsoever for a baby deliberately brought into this world seems to me utterly barbaric!

By contrast, abortion is absolutely moral and responsible. To stop the pregnancy and prevent the birth of a child who cannot be properly cared for shows wisdom—and understanding of the realities of life. The only life in an embryo is the woman's life within it. Until it can live a separate life, it is *not* a separate life. "Infallible" doctrines and dogmas simply wither away in the light of that fact. (Robertson 126)

3

Here are some reasons why friends of mine had abortions: they were in college and wanted to graduate. They were in graduate school or professional training and wanted to finish. They could not care for a child and keep their jobs. They were not in a relationship that could sustain parenthood at that time. They were not, in short, ready or able to be good mothers yet, although those who have children are good mothers now. Hard-hearted calculations of "convenience"? Only if you think that pregnancy is the price of sex, that women have no work but motherhood, and that children don't need grown-up parents.

The fact is, when your back is to the wall of unwanted pregnancy, it doesn't matter whether or not you think the fetus is a person. That's why, in this country, Roman Catholic women, who are less likely to use effective birth control, have a higher abortion rate than Jews or Protestants. Women do what they need to do in order to lead reasonable lives, and they always have.   (Pollitt 128)

4

We have learned a lot since that afternoon when our daughter Chrissie, just a few minutes old, took our family by the hand and gently led us into the world of the handicapped. Chrissie was born with Down syndrome. A mysterious bit of chromosomal protein created her almond-shaped eyes, squared-off ears, tiny nose, and low muscle tone. It created some mental and physical retardation, but we don't yet know how much. It also will require heart surgery. The odds are good, about twenty to one, that she will survive the surgery and will be restored to a practical normal existence. (Allison 146)

5

The issue of rape and incest must be faced squarely. Public funds should be denied for abortion in these cases because abortion is a great evil, and one that cannot be remedied. There is no second chance for an unborn child who has been dismembered. It is important to remember that a child of rape has not wronged its mother or anyone else.

It *is* unjust that a woman must carry to term a child conceived through rape. Yet it is a greater injustice to kill the child. Rape is a terrible act for many reasons, including brutality, humiliation, and the risk of venereal disease and unwanted pregnancy for the woman. It is also terrible because it risks placing the women in great temptation to kill. (Meehan 158)

6

Today, the reproductive rights of women are imperiled as never before. In July 1989—16 years after *Roe v. Wade* recognized women's constitutional right to abortion—the Supreme Court retreated from that historic ruling. It cleared the way for laws that victimize poor women seeking abortions. And in two subsequent rulings in June 1990, the court invited restrictions on teenagers' access to abortion.

It's easy to recognize *exactly* what the anti-choice zealots are doing by attacking society's most vulnerable target—the poor and the young—the anti-choice extremists are chipping away at the reproductive rights of *all* women. Plainly put, the Supreme Court rulings invite state governments to put fetuses first. And radicals in every state are trying to do just that. More than 200 anti-choice bills were introduced in the state legislatures between July 1989 and January 1991. . . . Fortunately, the reenergized pro-choice majority has defeated most of them. . . .

Eventually, one of these laws [or a similar one] will bring this battle back to the Supreme Court. (Wattleton 168)

7

The researchers further concluded that studies of the effects of multiple abortions "do not support a firm conclusion about whether the number of induced abortions per se produces any increased risk of adverse outcomes in subsequent . . . pregnancies." While some studies have linked multiple abortions to future difficulty in bearing children, the abortions most frequently implicated were performed using the D&C [dilation and curettage] method, which is rarely used for abortions in the United States today.

In short, while a single abortion does not appear to have any adverse implications for subsequent childbearing, less research has focused on multiple abortions performed using modern surgical procedures or second-trimester abortions. Additional research is necessary to determine whether they have an impact on a woman's future ability to bear healthy children. (Gold 193)

Works Cited

Allison, Christine. "A Child to Lead Us." *Human Life Review* Summer 1989. Rpt. in *Abortion: Opposing Viewpoints*. San Diego: Greenhaven, 1991. 146–51.

Booth, Wayne C. *Modern Dogma and the Rhetoric of Assent*. Chicago: U of Chicago P, 1974.

Bush, George. "The President's Speech." *New York Times* 17 Jan. 1991: A14.

D'Souza, Dinesh. "PC So Far." *Commentary* Oct. 1991. Rpt. in *Culture Wars: Opposing Viewpoints*. San Diego: Greenhaven, 1994. 85–91.

Fowler, Paul B. *Abortion: Toward an Evangelical Consensus*. Portland: Multnoma, 1987. Rpt. in *Abortion: Opposing Viewpoints*. San Diego: Greenhaven, 1991. 106–11.

Gitlin, Todd. "On the Virtues of a Loose Canon." *New Perspectives Quarterly* Summer 1991. Rpt. in *Culture Wars: Opposing Viewpoints*. San Diego: Greenhaven, 1994. 80–83.

Gold, Rachel Benson. *Abortion and Women's Health*. New York: Alan Guttmacher Institute, 1990. Rpt. in *Abortion: Opposing Viewpoints*. San Diego: Greenhaven, 1991. 188–93.

Meehan, Mary. *Human Life Review* Winter 1990. Rpt. in *Abortion: Opposing Viewpoints*. San Diego: Greenhaven, 1991. 158.

Pollitt, Katha. *New York Times Magazine* 20 Nov. 1988. Rpt. in *Abortion: Opposing Viewpoints*. San Diego: Greenhaven, 1991. 128.

Robertson, Constance. *The Religious Case for Abortion*, 1983. Rpt. in *Abortion: Opposing Viewpoints*. San Diego: Greenhaven, 1991. 126.

Swift, Jonathan. "A Modest Proposal." (1729) In *Jonathan Swift: Irish Tracts 1728–1733*. Ed. Herbert Davis. Oxford: Basil Blackwell, 1971. 109–18.

Wattleton, Faye. "Reproductive Rights *Are* Fundamental Rights." *Humanist* Jan.-Feb. 1991. Rpt. in *Abortion: Opposing Viewpoints*. San Diego: Greenhaven, 1991. 168–71.

"Who Says Good Writing Doesn't Pay?" *Quarterly Review of Doublespeak* Jan. 1984: 7.

CHAPTER

5

Knowing Your Audience

Suppose you live in a small community that has a well-defined historic district. All is peaceful until one day the churches in the old town begin opening their doors to the homeless, starting a soup kitchen and providing occasional cots. Soon people can be seen each evening streaming through the historic district to get hot meals. Suppose also that some local residents, annoyed because they think the churches' actions are undermining the peacefulness and safety of the historic area, have organized opposition and are planning to voice their concerns at the next board of commissioners meeting. You decide to attend the meeting and argue that feeding and caring for the homeless should take precedence over peacefulness of the town. You know that your words will be heard skeptically by the concerned citizens and favorably by the friends of the downtown churches. It is less clear how they will be heard by the commissioners. How would you plan your remarks so that they have the best chance of exerting favorable influence on the right people?

This conflict (which was played out recently in my town) illustrates the difficulty writers and speakers have in understanding an audience and in shaping communications to accommodate its nature. Arguments are seldom posed to clearly defined, homogeneous audiences. More often, at least in public debates, the cultural assumptions, religious beliefs, political convictions, and moral values of various segments of the audience will be diverse, if not antagonistic.

Analyzing an audience requires that the entire rhetorical context be understood. Not only should the audience be identified, but also the physical, psychological, and formal conventions that influence it. In the foregoing example, a speaker at the board of commissioners meeting would have to consider the constituencies (church supporters, opposed local residents, county commissioners) and also would have to determine the nature of such a meeting and the kind of discourse most appropriate for it. Since board meetings are frequently covered by reporters, it might also be well to think about how the remarks will look printed in the next day's newspaper. In the same way, writers of arguments for college courses need carefully to consider whether their writing is designed for students, professors, or a specified or unspecified outside audience.

Pitching arguments to an audience means knowing who that audience is and understanding something about the audience's values. Douglas Park, who has written extensively on audiences, feels there are two critical levels of audience analysis. First, writers need to consider the identity of the audience. In the case of the board of commissioners meeting this might include churchgoers, other residents, and elected officials. Second, writers need to consider how the audience views the specific subject matter and to anticipate how the intended thrust of the discourse will be received. This means that *why* some residents oppose attracting the homeless to their community needs to be considered as much as *why* the churches believe that their responsibility to the destitute warrants disrupting that community. One should also consider reasons that might compel the commissioners to side with one group over the other.

Park has suggested a series of questions that help the writer make some preliminary observations about audience. They are summarized here:

    I. What is the identity of the audience?

        A. What is the social relationship between the writer and audience?

        B. How does the discourse function in that relationship?

        C. What physical settings, conventions, and formats are associated with it?

    II. How does the audience view the writer's intentions?

        A. What is known or can be projected about the audience's attitudes and knowledge?

        B. To what extent are the audience's attitudes and purpose affected by its collective identity as an audience?   (484)

In the example under consideration, one might know that the audience has assembled to attend the scheduled meeting of the board of commissioners in the county courthouse, and that private citizens will be permitted to address the meeting (after waiting their turn among other constituents). One might assume that there will be at least three "camps" in the meeting: the church supporters, the other residents, and the commissioners. The first two groups may have acquired a collective identity, since members may have sought out one another independently before the meeting. All three groups can in turn be analyzed in terms of attitude, knowledge, and collective identity. Just as Cicero's Antonius considers the case from the point of view of his client, the judge, and his adversary, a speaker at the meeting might consider the position from the three points of view represented. For those supporting the churches, the issue is the responsibility to provide humanitarian aid to those in need. For the other residents, the issue is the peace and safety of their neighborhoods, and perhaps, property values. The commissioners are likely to be interested in all these issues, and in addition, will probably have concerns about the political volatility of the crisis and its implications for their reelection.

A writer does not always know what the audience believes, however; the audience may be so varied that no consensus is possible. When the president addresses the nation on live television, for instance, he must have a very broad notion of "audience." Lisa Ede and Andrea Lunsford, drawing on the work of Walter Ong, suggest that speakers frequently address this question by using verbal "cues" that would be familiar to a wide-ranging audience. For instance, President Jimmy Carter drew on a well-understood battle metaphor to advance his political aims when he claimed that his plan to fight inflation was the "moral equivalent of war" (161–62). Similarly, when General Norman Schwarzkopf referred to a movement of troops in the Persian Gulf War as a "Hail Mary" pass (Lakoff 9), he likened the proceedings to a football game. Such metaphors can be effective as long as they are understood by a large portion of the audience.

Audience and Level of Support Needed

Audiences are likely to accept, question, or reject assertions based on their own values and beliefs. Assertions that have a high level of acceptance probably don't need much support. An audience consisting of Weight Watchers probably won't need to be convinced that weight control has health benefits. Similarly, writing an argument critical of the Reagan years for an audience of Democrats does not require the kind of support needed for an audience of state Republican Committee members. Assertions that have low levels of acceptance, however, may need a considerable amount of support. The assertion that the Clean Air Act doesn't go far enough in protecting the environment probably will be rejected by an audience composed of industrial leaders.

Exercise 1

Outline how you would argue the following claims to each of the following audiences. What kinds of assertions would you need to make, and how much support would each of these assertions need?

1. To argue that smoking should be banned form all public locations:

    (a) to a general audience

    (b) to an audience of members of the tobacco lobby

    (c) to participants at a health fair

2. To argue that a toxic waste incinerator located in your county should be closed:

    (a) to an audience of concerned county residents

    (b) to a group of plant employees

    (c) to a group of dignitaries from across your state

3. To argue that we ought to have tough gun control policies:

    (a) to a general audience

    (b) to an urban audience

    (c) to an NRA audience

4. To argue that tuition should be increased at your college:

    (a) to parents

    (b) to trustees (or regents) of the college

    (c) to a group of students

Audience and Purpose of Argument

Considering audience may also affect the purpose of an argument. Let's say that John Q. Public wants to argue that the Democrats' proposed health care legislation represents a dangerous step toward socialized medicine. If he has been asked to speak before Young Republicans, he might go right to a call for action—"Write your congressperson!" If, however, he is speaking to Young Democrats, such a move might get him run off the stage. The speaker would have better chances of succeeding if he tried to show Young Democrats that the proposal is not as trouble-free as they had been led to believe. The same will be true in a written argument. If the audience is perceived to be hostile, the purpose of the argument may well need to be modified.

Linda Flower has written that there are three possible outcomes of argument (207). First, the arguer might win totally (this is very unlikely). It would be very surprising if a group of Republicans completely changed their minds about the quality of the Reagan years in response to a persuasive talk. Second, the arguer might get the audience to modify their beliefs. This is a much more achievable goal. It perhaps would be possible to get a group of Republicans to begin to see flaws in the Reagan record. Third, the arguer might discover that there has been no change at all. This, Flower finds, is the most common result of most arguments.

If arguments generally do nothing to change people's minds, why does anyone bother to argue? If the only purpose in argument were to bring the audience completely into accord with the persuader's views, there would indeed be very little compelling reason to argue, since this goal is almost never achieved. Surely, not all residents of the historic district will be persuaded to welcome the homeless with open arms. Many might not even accept the nonresidents grudgingly. In such cases, the purpose of the argument needs to be adjusted to meet the needs of the rhetorical situation.

Being persuasive means setting realistic expectations. One may have to be satisfied, for instance, with getting a majority of the local residents to see that the homeless people coming into their area are not quite as serious a threat as had been imagined. When it's unrealistic to expect an audience to embrace a claim, the purpose needs to be modified.

Exercise 2

> Look again at the four problems outlined in Exercise 1. How might the purpose be adjusted in arguing these issues to various audiences?

Audience and Tone

Adjusting the purpose to suit the rhetorical situation also means adjusting the tone to suit the audience. While supportive audiences may be relatively receptive to inflammatory language, a skeptical or hostile audience will not be easy on would-be persuaders who play fast and loose with tone. Attacking or belittling an audience will do little to establish a sense of trust and goodwill. In other words, effective persuaders don't attack those whom they oppose if they think the opposition may be part of the audience. No one who has any hope of changing his or her hearers' minds will say, "My opponents have stupid reasons for their biases."

Exercise 3

Read the following two paragraphs of Norm Allen's "Political Correctness and Right-Wing Propaganda." Whom do you assume his audience to be? What specific words or phrases in this passage reveal the writer's attitude toward his opponents? How does he characterize his opponents? How will the audience likely respond to his tone?

There is a debate raging among academics, media pundits, and ordinary citizens throughout the U.S. What is at issue is what is pejoratively referred to as "politically correct" (PC) speech and action. Examples of political correctness include the use of gender-neutral words which acknowledge the existence of women (e.g., "first year student" is used in place of "freshman"), the prohibition of racial slurs, the prohibition of sexist and homophobic speech and writing, etc.

The loudest and most obnoxious opponents of political correctness are mostly reactionary right-wingers with a political agenda of their own. Patrick Buchanan, George Will, William F. Buckley, William Bennett, Jeane Kirkpatrick, and other influential conservatives and neoconservatives have been adamant in their opposition to what they perceive as censorship on the part of school administrators and others in positions of power and authority. (100–103)

Rogerian Argument

One of the most important twentieth-century influences on the place of audience in argument is the rhetorical model based on the work of clinical psychologist Carl Rogers. Rogers believed that the best way to resolve conflict in therapy—and the best way to establish true communication—is to get each opposing party to completely understand the position of the other. "Real communication," he stated nearly a half century ago, "occurs . . . when we listen with understanding" or try "to see the expressed idea and attitude from the other person's point of view, to sense how it feels to him, to achieve his frame of reference in regard to the thing he is talking about" (285). In Rogers's method, before arguing a position, one must describe the position of the opponent in such a way that the opponent agrees that he or she has been understood correctly. Such a method establishes a common ground between people based on the development of goodwill between arguers and on the identification of each side with the other's point of view. Only after such common ground has been established does one move on to support an opposing claim. Before the opponent responds to the claim, he or she must describe the position just presented.

Rogerian argument works best with hostile or vulnerable audiences or in highly emotional contexts. Rogerian argument serves to defuse tense situations by assuring the audience that one has the members' best interests in mind. If the residents of the historic district believe the speaker understands what it's like to confront the problems of homelessness in their quiet neighborhoods, they will be more likely to listen to the speaker's position. Rogerian argument may also reveal why some disputes are unresolvable, especially in highly emotional arguments like those associated with abortion and capital punishment. If antiabortion and pro-choice advocates find it impossible to grant that the opposing position has any validity at all, there is little hope of finding any kind of common ground that would make communication (or the modification of beliefs) possible. All the advocates can do is rage at each other. This is one reason for considering arguments on these topics very carefully in terms of audience and purpose, and very frequently, a reason for avoiding them altogether.

Rogerian argument, even though it is nonconfrontational, does require a certain amount of risk. As Rogers observed, "you might find yourself influenced in your attitudes or your personality. This risk of being changed is one of the most frightening prospects most of us can face" (287). The change may not be bad, but if the only purpose is to win an argument, the Rogerian approach is not likely to lead to a clear-cut victory. The Rogerian system assumes that it is possible for the arguer to change every bit as much as the audience.

Of course, the Rogerian model can also be used in traditional adversarial argument. Even if one has no intention of being changed by the audience's position, it is still very valuable to analyze the audience's points of view. Indeed, the results of such an analysis may permit one to form an empathetic bond that opens the door to more effective persuasion.

Rogerian argument does have important application to written arguments. When the Rogerian system is used to develop claims, the audience's position or positions must be described first; this description is then used to establish a common ground, and finally, to develop the claim. It is most important to communicate to the audience that its points of view are not regarded judgmentally.

Refutation

Rogerian argument is important in yet another way. It serves to underscore the significance of refutation in argument. Refutation means understanding the opposing views and demonstrating why these views are flawed. By understanding the audience's reservations about the claim and responding to them, one can make any argument much stronger.

It's very difficult to overemphasize the importance of refutation to writing convincing arguments. Rogerian argument illustrates that tense atmospheres can be lightened by convincing an audience that they and their mind-set are clearly understood. Without a good refutation, the writer's self-assessment notwithstanding, the audience will likely think, "Too bad the writer doesn't know enough about the issue to know why *we* don't want to accept it." So, before stepping in front of the commissioners, a writer should determine that the strongest refutation to be faced is the fear of local residents that inviting the homeless into their neighborhoods at night will lead to increased danger and disruption.

Of course, we can't just identify a refutation and put it into the argument as though it were part of a formal class requirement. Addressing refutation means explaining why the refutation isn't sufficient. There are three possible ways to do this:

1. Oppose the claim directly

    In the board of commissioners meeting, one could claim that the fears of the local residents are unfounded. There will be no increase in vandalism or danger. In fact, crime might actually *decrease* because of the active presence of the Good Samaritans.

2. Parry the threat

    Take the refutation to its ultimate conclusion. "Are we to avoid all help to the less fortunate," one might argue, "when faced with the possibility of danger and vandalism? Of course not."

3. Concede (yes, but. . .)

    One might agree that there is indeed a possibility of increased danger and disruption but point out that it is a small price to pay for the benefits to be gained from addressing the needs of the less fortunate in the town.

Each kind of refutation responds directly to the concerns of the most hostile groups in the audience. They may not leave the meeting ready to invite the homeless into their living rooms, but they should realize that they've been heard, and that's the most important step right now. Only later can one hope to change their position.

Writing Assignment 1

Choose an issue of interest to you and write an argument to an audience of your classmates (or another specified audience). In writing the argument, here are some important things to keep in mind:

Arguability. The topic must be arguable. The best way to test a topic's arguability is to decide how easy it is to refute. Arguments that are either easy or impossible to refute aren't likely to be very strong. On the other hand, significant arguments will always have strong refutations.

Refutation. Once the refutation has been identified, don't hide it. Put it where people can see it. This will show that the writer (1) is well informed about the whole argument and (2) has considered the intelligence of the audience. It's possible (and often advisable) to organize the whole paper around its refutation—especially if the position is strong or particularly widely held.

Specifics. Simply stating that one position is wrong or another right won't convince anyone. It's important to use concrete examples. Get quotations, statistics, numbers—any form of data available to back up the assertions.

Audience. Finally, be kind to the audience. Assume that if not openly hostile, they are at least skeptical. That being said, stay in control of the language. If the audience's position is attacked too venomously or if they feel that their ideas are being belittled, there's no way they can be convinced, even if they are dead wrong.

Writing Assignment 2

Write an essay for submission to *Newsweek* modeled after the "My Turn" columns that appear regularly in the magazine. In this assignment be particularly conscious of the Rogerian model of argument. Before beginning, examine a few "My Turn" columns in recent issues to get a sense of format and tone. The key to this assignment is to write about something you are interested in or care about, something that makes a difference in your life. Here is one format you might consider:

1. Introduction
2. Fair statement of the opposing position
3. Statement of contexts in which that situation may be valid
4. Statement of your own position
5. Statement of the contexts in which your posittition is valid
6. Statement of how readers would benefit by at least moving toward your position

(This assignment was modeled on one designed by Dr. Carl Glover.)

Works Cited

Allen, Norm. "Political Correctness and Right-Wing Propaganda." *Freethought History* No. 5, 1983. Rpt. in *Culture Wars: Opposing Viewpoints*. San Diego: Greenhaven, 1994. (100–103).

Ede, Lisa. "Is Rogerian Rhetoric Really Rogerian?" *Rhetoric Review* 3 (1984): 40–48.

Ede, Lisa and Andrea Lunsford. "Audience Addressed/Audience Invoked: The Role of Audience in Composition Theory and Pedagogy." *College Composition and Communication* 35 (1984): 155–71.

Flower, Linda. *Problem-Solving Strategies for Writing*. 3rd ed. New York: Harcourt Brace Jovanovich, 1989.

Lakoff, George. "Metaphor and War." *Quarterly Review of Doublespeak* July 1993: 9–12.

Park, Douglas B. "Analyzing Audiences." *College Composition and Communication* 37.4 (1986): 478–88.

Rogers, Carl. "Communication: Its Blocking and Its Facilitation." Paper presented at 1951 Northwestern University Centennial Conference on Communications. Rpt. In Young, Richard E., Alton L. Becker, and Kenneth L. Pike. *Rhetoric: Discovery and Change*. New York: Harcourt, Brace, and World, 1970. 284–89.

6

Assembling the Written Argument

Once an issue has been analyzed, data gathered, an audience assessed, and a stance determined, one can begin thinking about committing the argument to writing. The more thoroughly the initial plans have been made, the easier will be the task of writing. Before putting pen to paper, however, it's a good idea to consider the logical structure of the argument. Writers must be very certain about the strength of each claim, the strength of the support for it, and the need for any qualifying considerations. In other words, every writer needs to think through a few things before arranging the argument on paper.

The Toulmin Model of Argument

One of the most influential methods for determining the structure of an argument was developed by British historian and philosopher Stephen Toulmin. In his 1958 book *The Uses of Argument*, and in a more recent work coauthored with Richard Rieke and Allan Janik, Toulmin describes a system of arguing based on his analysis of how arguments are carried out in real settings. Toulmin uses the terms "data," "warrant," and "claim" to describe the three critical parts of an argument. Since claims were the subject of Chapter 3, they are not explained further here. This section shows how claims can be tested and used to develop full arguments. Claims can be tested when they are examined along with the support (data) and generalizations (warrant). These three components provide a framework for the argument.

Data

"Data" refers to the evidence that is presented, the support for a claim. (In *An Introduction to Reasoning*, Toulmin et al. also refer to data as "grounds.") Someone arguing in favor of pesticides, for instance, might consider such factors as estimates of the projected crop losses if pesticides are not used, the results of scientific studies showing the limits of danger, and testimony from experts in the field. Someone arguing against disposable diapers might want to show statistics revealing that these throwaways make up 2 percent of all landfill refuse.

The Tools for Arguing section of this chapter will cover in more detail the kinds of evidence available to persuaders. For now it's enough to say that data or evidence can come from a wide range of sources including personal experience, statistics, authority, and narratives.

Warrants

Warrants are the generalizations that connect the data to the claim. In many ways they are similar to the hidden premise of the enthymeme in that both indicate larger assumptions which underpin the argument. If we claim that a proposed national health care plan would be a disaster because the cost would be borne primarily by middle-class Americans, and assuming the existence of sufficient evidence for that claim, the warrant would be stated as follows: "Health care plans that are financed primarily by middle-class Americans can be called 'disasters.'" The warrant is a generalization based on data and other forms of support called "backings."

Data, warrant, and claim can be diagrammed like this:

Data: Domestic auto prices have remained stable this year while the prices of imports have increased 15%.

Claim: Domestic autos are better values this year.

Warrant: Auto prices are good indicators of auto value.

Data: Senator Belfrey has the best economic plan of any candidate in this year's election.

Claim: Support Senator Belfrey.

Warrant: The candidate with the best economic plan should be supported.

Sometimes, however, arguments may be more complex. Perhaps the claims and warrants need to be qualified. Consider the following argument:

Data: Disposable diapers comprise 2% of landfill garbage.

Claim: Disposable diapers should be banned.

Warrant: Single items that comprise 2% of landfill garbage should be banned.

Qualifier: as long as suitable alternative modes of disposal are found.

In this case, the phrase "as long as suitable . . ." qualifies the warrant. Toulmin calls such phrases "modal qualifiers" when they apply to the warrant and "rebuttals" when they qualify the claim. We might, for instance, decide that the claim on diapers needs to be modified to permit exceptions. If someone invented a biodegradable diaper that promised to be safe for landfills, the argument could be rephrased something like this:

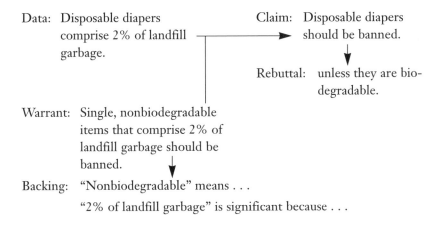

Data: Disposable diapers comprise 2% of landfill garbage.

Claim: Disposable diapers should be banned.

Rebuttal: unless they are bio-degradable.

Warrant: Single, nonbiodegradable items that comprise 2% of landfill garbage should be banned.

Backing: "Nonbiodegradable" means . . .

"2% of landfill garbage" is significant because . . .

Developing an effective argument demands that data, warrant, and claim be analyzed to see how much support, or backing, they will need to be convincing to a given audience. Notice that both data and warrant are also claims that may need their own support. The assertion that disposable diapers comprise 2 percent of landfill volume may or may not be an accepted fact. Similarly, the assertion that 2 percent of landfill volume presents a significant problem will likely need to be supported. In this example, the warrant probably needs two different kinds of support: a definition of nonbiodegradable and support for the assertion that 2 percent of landfill volume accounts for a significant amount of garbage.

The Toulmin method may be used to chart out arguments or to aid in understanding the arguments of others. The argument developed by Laura Weiss, analyzed in Chapter 2, contains both a warrant and qualifier (even though these may not have been articulated explicitly in the text):

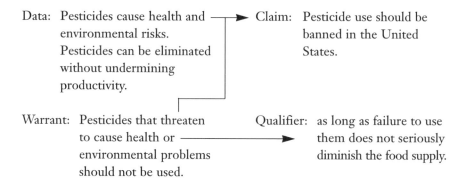

Data: Pesticides cause health and environmental risks. Pesticides can be eliminated without undermining productivity.

Claim: Pesticide use should be banned in the United States.

Warrant: Pesticides that threaten to cause health or environmental problems should not be used.

Qualifier: as long as failure to use them does not seriously diminish the food supply.

Although Weiss does not discuss her qualifier at length it is implied through her refutation (which will be examined shortly). Weiss's argument rests on the general principle that pesticides found to be harmful should not be used. According to the data of her argument, pesticides *are* in fact harmful and therefore it can be claimed that they should not be used.

Stasis and Warrants

Warrants, because they purport to be accurate generalizations, provide a common link between writer and audience. Notice that the warrant in Weiss's article mirrors the categories identified in Chapter 2: economic, health-related, environmental, and cultural. Of these four, Weiss focuses her warrant on health (whereas Bohmont concentrates on economic considerations). A good way to begin thinking of warrants is to return to the categories identified in planning arguments. To write a warrant, it's often useful first to consider which larger category is most important and then to explain its significance (in a single sentence).

For instance, someone who had identified environmental and technological factors as the most important reasons to support nuclear power might write a warrant something like this: "The best source of energy will be that which is technologically feasible while presenting the least potential for environmental damage." Someone who felt the topic required a modal qualifier might come up with the following warrant: "The best source of energy will be the most economically feasible as long as it doesn't do irreparable harm to the environment."

In writing arguments, it is equally important to consider the support needed for the warrant and the support needed for the claim. In the preceding example, the writer will want to ask, "Why is economic feasibility so important in deciding what to do about energy sources? What does 'irreparable harm to the environment' mean?" The writer might decide that it is necessary to show other sources of energy (solar, wind, thermal) to be economically infeasible or to demonstrate that some harm to the environment is unavoidable no matter what energy sources are used. These assertions will need careful development within the argument.

Exercise

Identify the warrant in each of the following arguments. Do the warrants need further backing? How would you develop such backing?

Data: Sixty percent of all Americans never read a book after they leave school.

Students' command of English grammar is much weaker now than it was twenty years ago.

Forty percent of Americans are functionally illiterate.

Claim: American education is not effective.

Data: Americans have the best health care in in the world.

The uninsured receive $10 billion in uncompensated health care annually.

Claim: There is no health care crisis.

Tools for Arguing

Organizing Arguments

The best organization for any argument will be one that seriously considers the stance of the audience, the strength of the evidence (or data), and the kind of claim that is being put forth. There is no single way to organize arguments effectively. In fact, the Toulmin model has a twofold advantage: it's flexible, and it allows for a number of different kinds of organization.

If the Toulmin model is being used, each of the argument's elements (data, warrants, and claims, with the appropriate qualifiers and rebuttals) may need serious attention, depending on audience and situation. To argue that disposable diapers should be banned, one might begin with data. Such an argument could conceivably include descriptions of dumps brimming with this form of waste, references to scientific studies of the chemical breakdown of the diapers, environmental studies of the consequences of the practice, and quotations from landfill management. But it might be necessary to discuss the warrant in some detail as well. The warrant "Single, nonbiodegradable items that comprise 2 percent or more of landfill garbage should be banned" might necessitate a discussion of the meaning of using 2 percent of landfill garbage. How much garbage is 2 percent? What percentage would be acceptable? It will probably also be necessary to spend some time developing a discussion of the rebuttal ("unless they are biodegradable"). What does "biodegradable" mean? Are biodegradable diapers available? Are they comparable in price to the other kind? The Toulmin model, then, offers a starting point to think about the conceptual organization of our arguments.

Introductions

It's very important in any kind of argument to get the trust of the audience immediately. While there's no surefire way to do this, here are a few possibilities. Some arguments begin with a story or an example:

> Eskimo mommies wrapped their babies' bottoms in peat moss. Plains Indian tribes used animal skins. In old Europe women knit wool flannel pants. And only one generation ago, we spent our infancies clad in cotton cloth. (Lyman 134)

> The sea winds were blowing onshore, cooling off a million weekend bathers escaping the hot August heat. But this breezy salvation for a sweltering southern California bothered the Coast Guard official. "You don't

want these winds when a tanker spills oil," he explained to me. "With winds like this, the skimmers are useless and the spill gets legs, real long legs." The fallback plan for this, I learned, would be to boom off three major ports, call off naval maneuvers, move some sea otters to onshore safety, and mobilize a work crew of 5,000 to hand-clean some 400 miles of the world's most photogenic coastline.   (Marx 134)

These openings are effective because they offer detailed descriptions of closely observed phenomena which pull the readers in and gain their trust in the positions that will follow. Telling stories and using examples are only two possible ways to begin. Some arguments get right to the point:

> Water problems are the result of misguided and misdirected human choices. They are not the product of physical or technical limitations of the resource itself.   (Felman 36)

The most important consideration in writing introductions is to find a way to engage the reader as soon as possible, revealing the claim clearly and early. As you read effective arguments written by other people, pay attention to what makes them work. Chapter 2 introduced two arguments on pesticides, one by Laura Weiss and one by Bert L. Bohmont. Let's return to them for a moment to see how they were organized. Weiss immediately gets the reader personally involved:

> If you're like most health-conscious Americans, you pay attention to the amount of cholesterol in your diet. But when was the last time you tried to calculate the amount of Captan you've eaten?   (67)

Having snared the reader's attention, Weiss defines her key term, Captan. She tells when the substance was introduced and what it is used for and discusses the government's willingness to permit its use and the danger inherent in this practice. Her claim—that we have become overdependent on pesticides—does not come until about a quarter of the way through the article.

Bert Bohmont begins with a story of the history of pesticides: "History records that agricultural chemicals have been used since ancient times; the ancient Romans are known to have used burning sulfur to control insects" (74). Only after establishing the long tradition of pesticide use does he move to his claim: that pesticides can be good for us.

Using Refutation (or Rebuttals)

Comparing the structure of these two arguments, the reader can see much in common despite obvious differences. Both are developed mainly in terms of factual data, relying less on appeals to authority (as opposed to personal experience). Both make extensive use of reports, statistics, and expert testimony. Both state their claims clearly, and both indirectly support their warrants (Weiss that human health is of paramount concern, Bohmont that food productivity is of paramount concern). However, while Bohmont makes considerable use of refutation (the whole second half of his article is devoted to it), Weiss devotes only one sentence to refutation. Why should this be true? Let's look more closely.

The bulk of Weiss's article develops a discussion of the dangers pesticides pose to the health of the nation. Buried in the paragraph beginning with the phrase "Many environmentalists," however, Weiss devotes a single sentence to the other side of the issue: "Conventional farming interests such as the Farm Bureau argue that large-scale food production is not possible without pesticides and that consumers need these chemicals to control germs, pests, and weeds" (68). The next sentence indicates that the U.S. Department of Agriculture reports an increasing number of farmers growing crops with no pesticides at all.

By contrast, nearly half of Bohmont's article is devoted to refutation. Beginning with the heading "Environmental Concerns," and continuing through the rest of the article, Bohmont responds to concerns that pesticides cause harm as well as provide benefit. He writes that environmental modifications must be seen in larger environmental contexts, that "injury and death to some life forms" is an unforeseen consequence, that we don't know everything about how pesticides decompose, and implies that the popular fear of pesticides is unwarranted. In fact, one might say that Bohmont structures his whole argument on refutation. What does this reveal about how Bohmont sees his audience (and how Weiss sees hers)?

While there's no easy answer to these questions (although they do merit discussing in class), we might conclude that Weiss believes her evidence to be so strong and so damning that in the face of the health dangers she identifies, no reasonable person could argue a counterposition. Bohmont, however, evidently knows how difficult it is to argue against the health of the community. His last paragraph concerning the fears of the community probably was written in response to fears he believes his readers have about pesticide use. To ignore these issues would be to invite the dismantling of his argument. The more highly charged the issue, the more imperative it is that the refutation be dealt with fairly and completely.

Writing Style

Using all the right data, stating the claim clearly, and supporting the warrants won't get the writer very far if the reader doesn't understand the prose or is put off by the writer's persona. In Chapter 4 we discussed the importance of having a clear sense of persona, and writing style is one important route to the creation of personas. Are the terms highly technical and abstruse, or are they simple? Does the writing sound like a conversation or a lecture? Is the organization clearly marked, or must the reader struggle to follow it? All these are questions of style. While there is no one correct style, a number of stylistic areas can be taken into consideration.

Simplicity and Directness

No one likes to tackle prose that seems to defy the reader to understand it. Look for ways to simplify language. Pay special attention to overuse of linking verbs—is, are, was, were. Ask yourself, "Can I find an active verb that will do the job of a multiword passive form?" Critique a sentence like "Pesticides are used by farmers who are concerned about their yield," by considering the effect of making it active: "Farmers concerned about their yield use pesticides." It won't be possible to eliminate all linking verbs—nor should one try—but finding active verbs to take their place is a good way to begin revising for economy.

Titles, Headings, and Transitions

Select titles carefully. Readers encounter titles before they ever begin working through arguments. Make the title clear, concise, and (if appropriate) witty. At the very least it should clearly reflect the argument contained in the writing.

Although arguments don't always use headings, sometimes these lines of displayed copy help the reader to follow the central points. Make sure to indicate whether headings are major or minor. Principal headings can be centered on the page and given their own lines; the less important ones can either be indented or printed flush with the left-hand margin. Just make sure that the relative weightings are clear.

Regardless of whether headings are used, the argument ought to contain clear transitions leading the reader from point to point. After finishing a draft, read through the opening lines of each paragraph to verify that one idea flows into another. Consider repeating key phrases in these lead sentences to help connect the ideas.

If the argument has been structured on the Toulmin model, the warrant, which provides the underpinning for the argument, can also be used to help keep the writer on track. For instance, in a paper arguing that Senator Belfrey should be supported for reelection because he has the best economic plan of any candidate, remember to show not only why this legislator's economic plan is the best but why an economic plan is important in evaluating any candidate. Discussing the importance of the economy in the election can supply a context for discussing Belfrey's economic plan.

Finding Data (or Evidence)

Support for arguments can come from a large number of sources, but certain kinds of evidence appear frequently in arguments. Appeals to facts, the opinions of others (or authority), personal experience, and narratives are four sources of evidence widely used by writers of arguments. Laura Weiss and Bert L. Bohmont make frequent use of appeals in the first two forms.

Facts

Both Weiss and Bohmont ask the reader to accept as fact a number of assertions about pesticides. Weiss reports that "In 1980, the National Cancer Institute found that Captan caused tumors in mice" (67). She says that the risks of pesticides include "seeping into groundwater, contaminating food supplies, and accumulating in the tissue of plants, animals, and people. [Pesticides] are capable of causing birth defects, genetic mutations, sterility, and cancer" (68). She further reports that the chemical Diazinon, which can be used on food crops, has been banned on golf courses because it kills birds. Bohmont writes that some pesticides decompose in the food chain and some persist and that pesticides require proper application and storage. All these statements are verifiable through sources external to the writers. They come from government reports, scientific studies, and common knowledge.

Opinion (Authority)

Frequently, effective evidence for arguments can be found in the informed opinions of others, especially those whose opinions count in the eyes of the audience. We trust such opinion all the time. When a surgeon general's report finds that smoking cigarettes is dangerous to human health or when a chief financial adviser for Merrill Lynch Investment Corporation forecasts a recession, writers are quick to bolster their claims with the words of such authorities. Appeals to authority, however, are only as good as the credibility of the source. Readers and writers always need to ask, "Whose opinion is it?" When the Merrill Lynch adviser comments on health risks from smoking or the surgeon general gives advice on the economy, the opinion isn't worth much. The opinion of a former secretary of state concerning foreign policy issues will probably carry more weight in an argument than the opinion of a microbiologist (although the scientist's opinion would be more persuasive in issues related to the food chain).

Determining the quality of authority isn't always this easy, however. In court cases that bring into question the sanity of the defendant, both the prosecution and defense may call psychiatrists to the witness stand. Since, however, these experts frequently offer contradictory opinions about the mental health of the defendant, the members of the jury must decide which authority to believe.

Even more trouble determining credibility confronts those weighing opinions taken from secondary sources. For instance, when a political columnist summarizes the position of an adversary, the reader might wonder whether the columnist has described her adversary's position accurately. It's much better not to take someone's word for the opinion of others if the original source can be found.

Authority is an important source of evidence and support, as long as it is trustworthy. Supermarket tabloids are famous for quoting "authorities" who either don't exist, didn't make the statements attributed to them in the context claimed by the publication, or aren't authorities on the issue at hand. Advertisers use celebrities to endorse products that don't necessarily relate to the stars' areas of expertise. Michael Jordon may be taken as an expert when he endorses basketball shoes, but when former baseball catcher Johnny Bench endorses a spray paint, the connection is not so clear. Toulmin et al. observe that the dubious validity of some celebrity endorsements lies in a failure to "establish an adequate *foundation* for the authority" (230).

Both Weiss and Bohmont make frequent use of authority. When Bohmont writes that agricultural advocates like the Farm Bureau "argue that large scale food production is not possible without pesticides and that consumers need these chemicals to control germs, pests, and weeds" (68), he is using the Farm Bureau as an authority to support his claim. Similarly, when Weiss writes that the "U.S. Department of Agriculture estimates that 30,000 farmers are now raising crops without chemicals or are close to eliminating their use, and other experts say the numbers range from 50,000 to 100,000" (68), she assumes that the reader will accept this federal agency as a knowledgeable authority on pesticide use.

Personal Experience

Personal experience can also be a persuasive source of evidence. Imagine writing an argument opposing the use of pesticides from the perspective of having witnessed aerial crop dusting and observed the effects of this practice on the animals, people, or water supply in an area. These observations could be an important source of information. Patricia J. Williams, in "Blockbusting the Canon," uses her experience as a black woman confronting a racially insensitive statue of a black student at the University of North Carolina to argue that political correctness is justified. She begins her piece by saying

> I am about to turn 40 years old. While I suppose that makes me a Baby
> Boomer, I have always thought of myself as a Little Rocker: my earliest
> memories include the integration of the schools in Little Rock, Arkansas,
> by children just about my age.   (93)

Williams's argument is effective in part because she is immediately affected by
the insensitivity of the statue. She has witnessed not only the offending piece but
also the context in which the piece is offensive. That personal understanding
becomes the basis for her argument.

Narratives.   Everyone loves stories. Stories keep our attention, and they can
be valuable ways to make points and teach lessons. Telling the story of a small
animal affected by pesticides (as long as the tale is compelling and not just a sen-
timental setup) can be a powerful way to begin an argument. Indeed, it might be
the entire argument. Many arguments are based almost entirely on narratives. A
story that describes an ecological paradise soon to be bulldozed into oblivion
hardly needs to argue that replacing the idyllic scene with a parking garage is a
bad thing.

Narratives can go wrong very easily, however. A story that's trite or simplistic
may have an effect opposite that intended by the writer. To be effective, stories
need to be well told and to the point. It's also a good idea to keep them brief, to
ensure that the audience doesn't become confused with the narrative and forget
what the writer is trying to say.

Kinds of Evidence

Arguments written for different contexts usually need different kinds of evidence. This is especially true in academic fields. In biology, for instance, direct
observation is an acceptable way to generate data. In literature, however, direct
observation outside the text may not be valued as highly as close textual analysis
(this will in itself differ from context to context). In psychology one might design
an experiment to test data, but in a history class one is more likely to test data
against original sources.

The kind of evidence used (authority and facts) and the method of support
used (stories, analogies, the Toulmin system) will be equally important in creating the argument. As we move into the next chapters we'll see how these methods of support can be used in writing arguments for two specific kinds of writing:
evaluations and proposals.

Writing Assignment

Write a position paper based on an issue of your choice, aimed at an audience of your peers. The paper might begin with a discussion of the perspectives from which the issue may be viewed. For this part of the assignment, think of the questions of stasis covered in Chapters 1 and 2. What are the central categories of issues involved in the larger issue?

After the issue has been analyzed, decide on a claim and on a method of support. For this part of the assignment it will be helpful to consider the Toulmin method discussed in this chapter. Think carefully about the data, and decide which evidence will be most effective.

Before you begin writing, think about the audience. What might be your classmates' position(s) on the issue? Will they be uncommitted or fairly united in their beliefs? Finally, decide on a goal for the argument. Do you want the audience to change their minds or to become more committed to a presently held belief? Determining a goal ahead of time will help you frame your argument to get the best results.

Works Cited

Bohmont, Bert L. *The Standard Pesticide User's Guide*. Englewood Cliffs, NJ: Prentice Hall, 1990. Rpt. in *The Environmental Crisis: Opposing Viewpoints*. San Diego: Greenhaven, 1991. 74–79.

Felman, David Lewis. *Water Resources Management: In Search of an Environmental Ethic*. Baltimore: Johns Hopkins UP, 1991. Rpt. in *Water: Opposing Viewpoints*. San Diego: Greenhaven, 1994. 36–38.

Lyman, Francesca. "Diaper Hype." *Garbage* Jan.–Feb. 1990. Rpt. in *The Environmental Crisis: Opposing Viewpoints*. San Diego: Greenhaven, 1991. 134–39.

Marx, Wesley. *The Frail Ocean*. Old Saybrook, CT: Globe Pequot, 1991. Rpt. in *Water: Opposing Viewpoints*. San Diego: Greenhaven, 1994. 134–38.

Toulmin, Stephen. *The Uses of Argument*. Cambridge: Cambridge UP, 1958.

Toulmin, Stephen, Richard Rieke, and Allan Janik. *An Introduction to Reasoning*. 2nd ed. New York: Macmillan, 1984.

Weiss, Laura. "Killer Compounds." *The Public Citizen* Jan.–Feb. 1988. Rpt. in *The Environmental Crisis: Opposing Viewpoints*. San Diego: Greenhaven, 1991. 67–72.

Williams, Patricia. "Blockbusting the Canon." *Ms.* Sept.–Oct. 1991. Rpt. in *Culture Wars: Opposing Viewpoints*. San Diego: Greenhaven, 1994. 93–99.

7

Writing the Evaluative Argument

Sometimes arguments, or parts of arguments, take the shape of evaluation. Evaluation, which occurs whenever two or more things are compared with each other or to an external standard, differs from other argumentative strategies in requiring the identification and ranking of criteria.

For instance, before buying a primary transportation vehicle one might consider pint-sized sports cars, four-door sedans, and vans. This three-choice field forces the buyer to select from among a number of competing alternatives. The basis (or bases) for choosing the type of vehicle to buy provides the *criteria* for the decision. Once the focus has been narrowed to a few potential models, a number of questions need to be asked about each model: "How much does it cost?" "What's the gas mileage like?" and "What kind of repair record does it have?"

Thus model, price, repair record, and mileage are criteria that will help one to make the decision, but answering those questions won't necessarily reveal what car to buy until it has been decided which criteria are the most important. At some point those criteria must be weighted against each other. In all likelihood the evaluator will find a car that meets most of the stated needs—for example, it's sporty, dependable, and fuel efficient. Unfortunately, it probably costs twice as much as the buyer had budgeted. Now it will be necessary to weigh the advantages of the final candidate against its single disadvantage and ask "Is the car worth the debt?"

Evaluations occur both as the focus of arguments and as part of larger arguments. The review, for instance, is an argument developed largely through evaluation (although it makes a good use of other techniques as well, especially description). At other times positions will be evaluated as part of larger arguments. Proposing the establishment of a soup kitchen will likely result in the need to evaluate the pluses and minuses of several locations. Whether one is writing a formal review or using evaluation for some other ends, the establishment of clear criteria is essential.

Let's begin with a simple example. Suppose Liz, a student, plans to apply to graduate school. Before sending her deposit off with the application form, she should ask, "How are graduate schools evaluated?" She might list quality of the faculty, quality of the academic program, employment history for graduates, and location. Examining these in turn, Liz may find that each criterion will need its own evaluation. For instance, to evaluate the quality of the academic programs, she might examine the quality of the faculty, the number and kind of courses (which will be listed in the college catalog), the size of the library, and reviews of the program (found in graduate school handbooks). Location might be evaluated by identifying such factors as proximity to major cities (if that is deemed important) and the area of the country in which the university is situated. The quality of the faculty might be evaluated by looking in the catalog to see where the members of the teaching staff received their degrees, and what fields are represented. The criteria identified—quality of the faculty, academic program, placement history, and location—must be weighted, or ranked, before a firm decision can be made. It could be that location is of paramount concern or that size of library matters little. Ranking will reveal which criteria to evaluate most seriously.

Evaluation occurs in more sophisticated arguments as well, although identifying the right criteria is likely to be more problematic in these arguments. In evaluating the efficacy of punishments for serious felonies (as a first step in writing an argument about capital punishment), the writer needs to ask some questions that will help generate criteria:

1. Does the punishment serve as an effective deterrent to crime?
2. Is it ethical? (Is it wrong for the state to take life or to imprison someone permanently? What if mistakes are made?)
3. Can the punishment be a tool of repression?
4. Is it constitutional?

Four criteria can be distilled from these questions: (1) effectiveness as a deterrent, (2) morality, (3) politics, and (4) constitutionality. Each of these will need to be analyzed and ranked against the others. For instance, what if the writer found that capital punishment, though an effective deterrent to crime, is unconstitutional? Then it would become necessary to ask whether it is more important to effectively punish criminals or to have carefully articulated and consistent governmental policies. Creating such an argument entails evaluation of the relative merits of effectiveness and constitutionality.

Exercise 1

Establish criteria that could be used to evaluate each of the following:

1. A restaurant
2. A personal computer
3. A national health care plan
4. A concert

Evaluating Issues

When one is assigned to cover one side of a polemic issue like capital punishment or abortion, time spent in evaluating counterpositions can often reward the writer by indicating ways to gain the support of audiences already favoring the opposing view. Polemic issues are those that tend to get people strongly supporting one of two sides: either capital punishment is wrong or it's right; either abortion is wrong or it's not. Polemic issues are particularly difficult to argue because people often hold their positions very firmly. The best approach probably is to start by establishing criteria for what one wants to accomplish. For instance, to argue about punishment for serious felonies, one might establish that the means selected should be just, humane, and effective as a deterrent. Then one could discuss whether capital punishment meets those criteria. Evaluating the soundness of the various positions provides a way to let the audience know that they are understood. It's another way to use refutation to advantage.

Evaluation also appears as part of more complex arguments. Let's consider the issue of capital punishment in more detail. Two essays on capital punishment, one by Robert W. Lee and one by Matthew L. Stephens, are included at the end of this book. They will provide a good starting point for the discussion. Before examining them, however, let's develop a set of criteria for determining when, if ever, capital punishment should be applied.

Exercise 2

Why should the death penalty be included in the penal codes of the states that permit it? Why should it be removed? After listing as many reasons as possible, try to distill a set of criteria for the application of the death penalty. Then identify the criteria used by Lee and Stephens in their articles.

Although Lee and Stephens use very similar criteria to evaluate the efficacy of capital punishment, their weighting and application of these criteria lead to two very separate positions. For instance, both authors address the question of deterrence by asking whether the death penalty actually prevents anyone other than the person executed from committing violent crimes. Both address the issue of cost-effectiveness, and both ask whether the death penalty can be applied judiciously. For this last criterion, Lee brings up the question of whether the death penalty discriminates on the basis of race or gender. Stephens describes the criteria of judiciousness by asking two questions: (1) Can capital punishment be applied equally under the law? (2) Do death-row inmates have adequate legal representation? Lee, however, raises a question not addressed by Stephens: Is the punishment deserved? Thus the criterion of justice has a place in Lee's argument.

Even though the two writers identify very similar criteria, their rankings are quite different. Lee gives most weight to the criterion that Stephens leaves out: justice. For Lee, the most important issue is whether the criminal deserves the punishment. The second most important criterion seems to be cost-effectiveness; the third most important is whether the punishment has a discriminatory effect; and finally, effectiveness as a deterrent is considered. Lee actually undermines the argument based on deterrence with his argument for justice. "Deterrence," he writes, "should never be considered the *primary* reason for administering the death penalty" (100). So neither writer pins his arguments on this issue.

For Stephens, the most important point seems to be whether the death penalty can be applied equally and with adequate legal representation (for simplicity I am treating these two matters as a single criterion). Cost-effectiveness and usefulness as a

deterrent follow. Thus, we can chart out their criteria something like this:

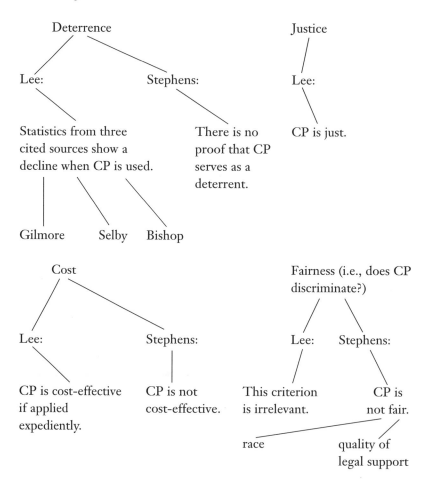

Charting the arguments in this way also allows the reader to rank
the criteria as Lee and Stephens see them:

Lee
1. Justice
2. Cost-effectiveness
3. Fairness
4. Deterrence

Stephens
1. Fairness
2. Cost-effectiveness
3. Deterrence

Writing the evaluative argument requires many of the same techniques found in other arguments. Notice that Lee makes fairly extensive use of refutation in his argument (103). The section headed "Lifetime to Escape" addresses the assertion that life imprisonment is an adequate substitute for capital punishment and the charge that is Stephens's central argument, namely, that capital punishment discriminates against minorities. Lee, in fact, turns the second argument around by suggesting that capital punishment discriminates against men (since so few women are executed).

Exercise 3

At the end of his article, Lee cites a sociological study showing that "women who cried during trials had a better chance of getting away with murder and avoiding the death penalty." He then suggests that the National Organization for Women should do something about "this glaring example of sexist 'inequality' and 'injustice'" (104). Is this suggestion serious? Why does the author use it? Does it make his argument more persuasive?

In the fifth paragraph of his article, Stephens calls death-row prisoners "poor and oppressed children of God who become the victims of our society's anger and need for revenge" (106). What is the emotive effect of this passage? Does it make his argument more persuasive?

Exercise 4

What are the criteria implied in the following passage? What does the tone imply?

There are three good things about capital punishment. One, the killer gets to experience the same fear and agony he inflicted on others. Two, the recidivism rate for executed murderers is zero. Three, electricity (or rope or bullets or drugs) is cheaper than room and board.

The average time served on a life sentence in the United States is about six years. Murderers can usually find ways to get out of prison. So far, none has gotten out of a grave. (Reece 103)

Role of Audience in Evaluation

Audience plays an important role in evaluating, just as it does in other forms of argument. In addition to forcing a consideration of the audience's stance, evaluation requires a decision about the extent to which the audience accepts the writer's criteria. In arguing in favor of capital punishment to a group of opponents of the death penalty, one might begin by considering whether this audience would accept deterrence as an important criterion and, if so, whether such listeners believe that capital punishment can serve as a deterrent. Even people who accept deterrence as a criterion might not agree that capital punishment is sufficiently effective as a deterrent to warrant its use. The same use of bias to rationalize the rejection of one of the writer's criteria might be encountered by a debater arguing against capital punishment to a group of supporters of the death penalty. Such an audience might well accept the idea that justice or fairness is a proper criterion, but one would not be likely to find acceptance of the assertion that the death penalty is inherently unfair.

Special Problems in Evaluation

Writing About Works of Art

Evaluating works of art presents special problems because the criteria for discussing art may seem self-generated. A person may admire a work by Southwest painter Jim Rabby, but how can this viewpoint be "argued" other than by saying "I like this canvas"? Few arguments are so difficult to prove convincingly because as a rule they appear to be motivated purely by personal taste: "It's good because I say so."

In my office I have a hand-painted coffee mug purchased at a craft show; it has a unique design—the bottom of the cup slants at an angle above the base. I often bring the mug into class and ask my students to evaluate it. They ask me questions: Is it functional? (No, the coffee spills easily, and the slanted bottom prevents the coffee from staying hot for more than a few seconds.) Was it expensive? (Yes, I paid $15 for it several years ago.) The students can clearly see that the piece is handcrafted and colorful, but they invariably disagree on whether these qualities make it a good mug. I then pull out a mug of the sort purchased from any dime store. It's white, functional, and characterless. But it is easily manipulated and keeps coffee hot. Which is the better mug? Of course, the purpose of a coffee mug must be determined before the criteria can be evaluated. Is it more important for the item to be aesthetically pleasing or functional? Criteria for "aesthetically pleasing" might include color, balance, design, and material. Functionality might be evaluated in terms of heat resistance, convenience, and durability.

It's particularly important that the criteria be clear and persuasive. A critic who dislikes one movie (or believes another is the greatest movie ever made) needs to think carefully about *why* a given work is so good or bad. In fact, asking why will probably generate further criteria. Is the acting good or bad? Is the screenplay engaging? Is the pacing effective, or does the story seem to drag?

Creating lists of criteria for aesthetic issues isn't much different from establishing criteria for social issues. In an art appreciation class some of these criteria will be given: form, color, design. In a literature class students may be asked to respond to characterization, plot structure, or writing style. Some of these criteria have been developed over the centuries. Aristotle's claim that a tragic character needs to possess a fatal flaw is still a criterion for evaluating works in the genre called tragedy.

Writing the Review

Writing reviews of movies, CDs, books, and restaurants is fun and provides an easy way to get published. All types of review have special conventions, however, and these are worth examining. First let's consider purpose. Reviews are designed not only to convince the reader that the writer's opinion is correct but to provide information about the thing being reviewed. Many people read reviews to become well informed about issues, authors, and artists, not just for recommendations on what to see or buy. That is why description and summary play such important roles in the review.

Book and movie reviews always contain some idea of the *plot* or *general theme* (although they never give the ending away). They might also contain references to similar works, authors, or musicians.

Reviews always have *sharp detail*. Book reviewers quote poignant passages; record reviewers comment on specific cuts or even passages within songs; movie reviewers quote dialogue or try to describe scenes cinematically. Restaurant reviewers report whether the avocado came from California or Florida and what spices went into the gumbo. Professional reviewers of movies go to screenings prepared to record their observations.

Reviews also tend to be lively, even when they are published in scholarly journals. Frequently the writers make personal comments and tell stories. It's especially important to come up with opening lines lively enough to hold the reader's attention. The review, perhaps more than any other form of argument discussed in this book, is a form of entertainment; the pace must move quickly enough to be entertaining, and the tone, likewise, must be designed to engage the reader's interest.

Reviews are always based on *criteria*, sometimes explicit and sometimes implicit. Good reviewers don't simply write that they like or dislike what they're reviewing. In addition to discussing the quality of food, restaurant reviewers may consider the efficiency of the staff, the breadth of the menu, the size of the dessert tray, and the cost of the meal. A CD reviewer may take into consideration the total time recorded as well as the quality of the music. All these are criteria.

Reviews frequently present a *balanced* approach to evaluation. Very seldom is a review so critical that no praise can be found; and even the most fulsome praise is generally leavened with objections of some type. There is a reason for this. The author of reviews that consist only of praise may be thought to lack critical distance, perhaps to be incapable of objective judgment. Thus reviewers who wish to praise a work of art enthusiastically always find something (even something very minor) to criticize. In the same way, reviewers who wish to pan a work frequently find something praiseworthy ("this movie was based on a great idea, but . . .") to persuade the reader that the review isn't just a hatchet job. It's also important not to make unsupportable claims. Instead of writing that a movie "reached the heights of greatness," it is better to stay as close to immediate observation as possible.

Reviews are invariably *short*, sometimes consisting of a single paragraph. They seldom run more than five to seven typed pages, largely because editors often want to include several reviews in a publication. Here is an example from the "CD Reviews" section of the magazine *Downbeat.*

Without a doubt, vocalist Gabrielle Goodman has polished pipes and a bold delivery, but on *Travelin' Light* . . . what she fails to do is travel lightly. Actually, what sets this album apart is the company she keeps, sometimes serving to show her up in terms of subtlety rendered. On the rolling Latin pulse of "Cherokee," for instance, star soloist Gary Thomas puts his tenor sax through some measured but intense paces, while Goodman goes for easy crowd-pleasing high-register gusto. On a cool reading of "Over the Rainbow," Kevin Eubanks lays down some tender guitar lines for a vocal that, while assured, gets lost in soulful abandon and overkill. On this set of standards and Latinesque originals, Goodman impresses the most when she's not going over the top.   (Woodward 44)

What criteria can you identify in this brief review? Notice that the writer does not try to say everything about the CD, nor does he confine himself to general evaluative comments. Woodward creates a balance between general observations ("polished pipes" and "bold delivery") and more concrete references to facets of the delivery of specific songs.

The evaluation contained in a review ought also to be *clear*. No one wants to see, at the end of a review, "Let the reader decide." The reviewer is supposed to take a clear stand. A review doesn't have to be one-sided, but the successes and failures of the work in question must be clearly articulated in terms of the reviewer's criteria.

Writing Assignments

1. Write a print media review of a current book, movie, or dramatic production. Be sure to indicate the periodical for which the review is intended: a school paper, a local paper or magazine, *Newsweek*, the *New York Times*. Before writing the review, examine some similar reviews in the publication selected to find out a little about the audience. A brief summary or description of the piece being reviewed makes a good beginning, but get to the point quickly (and never give away the ending). Be sure to consider what criteria should be used and weight them carefully.

2. Evaluate the courses required for graduation at your college, either in your major or as part of the general studies requirement. For this assignment you'll need to develop criteria to decide what constitutes an effective major or general studies program. (*Hint:* Examine programs in schools similar to your own.)

3. Compare two literary works or two works of art. Explain why you are comparing them and how you decided on your criteria.

4. Write an argument supporting (or opposing) abortion, capital punishment, or euthanasia. In your essay try to identify and evaluate the various possible positions on the issue.

Works Cited

Lee, Robert W. "Deserving to Die." *The New American* 13 Aug. 1990. Rpt. in *The Death Penalty: Opposing Viewpoints*. San Diego: Greenhaven, 1991. 98–104.

Reece, Charlie. *Conservative Chronicle* 15 Feb. 1989. Rpt. in *The Death Penalty: Opposing Viewpoints*. San Diego: Greenhaven, 1991. 103.

Stephens, Matthew L. "Instrument of Justice or Tool of Vengeance?" *Christian Social Action* Nov. 1990. Rpt. in *The Death Penalty: Opposing Viewpoints*. San Diego: Greenhaven, 1991. 106–12.

Woodward, Josef. *Downbeat* Aug. 1994. 44.

8

Writing the Proposal

Perhaps no kind of argument demands a clearer sense of audience and purpose than the proposal. Proposals aim at getting something done and usually stipulate who will do it and the conditions under which it will be accomplished. Proposals suggest that something be done in a specified manner, with specified facilities, within a given timetable, often (though not always) for a specified cost. They are nearly always addressed to people in positions of authority (a supervisor might write a proposal for the CEO, but not the other way around), and they are usually very detailed and complete, especially if the costs are high.

Proposals are used frequently in business and industry, although issue-oriented proposals relating to public policy make use of many of the same argumentative strategies. Because of this, it will be helpful to look at the technical proposal by itself in some detail. Technical proposals often concern physical or programmatic changes that require funding. In fact, cost often becomes the central issue that proposals must justify. Many wonderful-sounding proposals have gone awry because the designated reader thought the cost wasn't worth the benefits.

Not all proposals are technical, however. Sometimes proposals respond to larger cultural and political issues. One could propose that a state pass tougher gun control legislation, that the National Endowment for the Arts be defunded (or more generously funded), or that the United States renegotiate its trade agreements with Japan. While proposals on these topics have much in common with technical proposals, they differ in that they often omit detailed suggestions for implementing the desired changes. They stop short of saying that Senator Bobsled ought to spearhead the drive for gun control legislation or that the president ought to call a trade summit with Japan to renegotiate tariffs. Modified general proposals tend to concentrate on the problem and point toward (but not detail) a solution.

Almost by definition, proposals are controversial. Suppose I want my college to install new lights in a parking lot. If the idea were so transparently excellent that no one could ever oppose it, wouldn't I simply walk into the office of the head of maintenance (or possibly another administrator) and say "Let's do it!"? Similarly, if the president of the college wanted the lights, no proposal would be necessary since he or she would not expect opposition in this relatively trivial matter.

The need to write a proposal at all implies that the outcome is not clear. Perhaps the lights can be installed, perhaps not. Maybe the administrators don't think the lights are necessary, or perhaps they believe that the expense of putting them up will not be offset by the benefits claimed.

Because of this, proposals need very clear planning in terms of audience and purpose, and the details included must be carefully selected. Who, for instance, should receive the proposal on parking lot lights? It should go to the person at the college best able to make that decision—and this official will likely differ from institution to institution. At my college the provost would likely decide, in consultation with the president and the head of maintenance (who holds the purse strings). Writing such a proposal to the provost means thinking about what the provost's responsibilities are and how accepting this proposal could make the incumbent a better provost. I could argue, for instance, that installing the lights would increase the safety of students, staff, administration, and faculty or that it might prevent future lawsuits. All these considerations are within the purview of the provost's office.

Proposal writers need to be very clear on lines of responsibility. It isn't very helpful to send a brilliantly written and argued proposal to the wrong person. At best, it wastes time: if I had written first to the president of the college or to the director of maintenance, I would have had to wait in each case until the incorrect addressee had rerouted my proposal to the provost.

Exercise 1

To whom might you send the following proposals? Why?

1. Remodeling a college's newspaper office.
2. Adding (or dropping) a required course to a department's curriculum (or to the college's general studies curriculum).
3. Instituting a barking dog ordinance for a county.

Organizing the Proposal

Stating the Problem

Proposals, especially when they are on technical topics, tend to move the reader through a specific line of reasoning. Because of their controversial nature, proposals that respond to a stated need of the reader are far more likely to be received favorably than those that don't affect the reader personally or professionally. A request for parking lot lighting may elicit a knee-jerk reaction ("too expensive") unless the reader is convinced that *not* installing the lighting will create even more problems. Thus it is usual to begin with a discussion of the problem. This might call for some background information. Has lack of lighting led to trouble in the parking lot in the past? A check with security or with the dean's office could yield answers. Perhaps a number of cars have been broken into, or maybe security has had reports of assaults. Even if no specific incident has been logged, there might be a recognized potential for such difficulties.

The problem section of the proposal should be developed with sufficient clarity and force to convince the reader of the proposal that something needs to be done. Creating this sense of need is one of the most important aspects of proposal writing. The reader must come to believe that a problem exists. Rejecting the proposal won't make a problem go away. It will just delay the consequences. If the reader believes that a problem exists, it will be much easier to argue for the acceptance of a plan that addresses it.

In the problem section, as in the body of the proposal, the questions of stasis may provide clues to organization. For instance, it's good to develop categories as more information is generated. Let's imagine that a writer finds the following problems at a college:

1. A car parked in the lot was broken into last month.
2. Security has found people who neither attend nor work at the college walking through the lot at night.
3. Although no assaults have been reported in this particular lot, a student was harassed in a neighboring lot.

In addition, the writer discovers the following background information:

4. The lot provides parking for people (from the college and community) attending concerts and dramatic productions.
5. Students and faculty use the lot for night classes.

Given these facts, the problem section could be divided into two categories: safety of students and faculty; safety to community. By addressing each category in some detail, it is possible to determine what qualities these problems have and to introduce a series of issues: how serious the problems are, and how serious the audience thinks they are (are they life threatening or merely inconvenient?).

Stating the Solution

In technical proposals the solution is often stated in one or two sentences, sometimes at the very beginning of the proposal. In any case, it's often useful to give the solution its own heading and paragraph rather than bury it in the text. The reader needs to know early and clearly exactly what is being proposed.

The Body of the Proposal

The main part of the proposal is normally devoted to explaining exactly how the writer aims to accomplish what is proposed or how other people will be deployed to these ends. Depending on the kind of proposal, here are some important things to consider.

Facilities.   What college facilities will be required? This section might not be needed for the case of parking lot lighting unless the hardware would be designed or assembled by the college. However, someone proposing a concert series would have to state the desired location for the performances, estimate the costs of renting the building and the sound equipment, and probably tell who is responsible for insurance.

Personnel.   This section will describe the personnel needed to install and maintain the lights. Obviously, writing such a section for the case of the parking lot lights will require talking to the director of maintenance to find out how much labor will be involved. The appendix of the proposal might include verification from the director of maintenance that there are personnel available to do the job.

Schedule.   Be as specific as possible about the timetable. Are the lights to be installed over the summer or during the school year? Will the project be completed in stages or all at once? Will additional maintenance be needed? If so, how often?

Cost.   In most technical proposals cost is the most important factor—at least it's the reason most proposals are rejected. Be clear about the cost of the proposed changes—and who will bear it. It's best to itemize costs and provide some backup for the figures. For instance, it would be a very good idea to get written estimates on cost from the vendor of the lights (for the materials) and from the director of maintenance (for labor).

Conclusion.   In a traditional proposal the conclusion returns to the problem section and argues that solving the problem as stipulated in the proposal is worth the cost. In this example, one would state that the safety to students, faculty, and members of the community is well worth the money that would be needed to install the parking lot lights.

Appendix.   It's very important to bolster a proposal with concrete support for its claims. Sometimes backup data belong in the body of the proposal itself, but at other times such data serve the writer better in an appendix. Rather than cluttering the cost section of a proposal with a five-page estimate for expenditures, it may be preferable to break this material into separate documents (labeled "Exhibit 1," "Exhibit 2," etc.). That way, when cost items are referred to, the writer need only add "(see Exhibit 1)."

Refutations in Proposals

Refutations are critical to successful proposals as they are in any kind of argument. One of the major refutations will likely be cost, but there can be others as well. Perhaps the provost believes that since there have been no assaults in the parking lot, it is not necessary to spend money on installing lights. Maybe he thinks that the evening traffic in the lot doesn't justify all the fuss, or that the cost would be truly prohibitive. Neglecting to anticipate and address such assumptions could undermine the proposal. As in other arguments, there are a number of ways to respond to refutation. The writer might show that the high cost of the lights will be offset by the overall benefits of the plan. In any case, the proposal must identify and respond to all the pertinent refutations.

Clarity of Proposal Organization

Because a proposal needs to be immediately clear, it's a good idea to use headings for the separate sections. If headings aren't used, the material must be organized and presented to ensure that readers can follow the train of thought effortlessly.

Modified General Proposals

Not all proposals respond to technical problems. Some address more complex issues: "capital punishment ought to be abolished" or "the Clean Air Act ought to be strengthened." Even these more general proposals, however, are likely to

employ similar psychological movement. Modified proposals frequently emphasize the problem section without going into excessive detail about the mechanism
by which the action would be completed. Proposing that Yucca Mountain,
Nevada, be used to store nuclear waste probably can be done without an in-depth
discussion of how the waste is to be transported to the site or contained once it
gets to the mountain. It is enough in the modified proposal for the writer to create a real sense of need (the problem) and then point toward a solution.

Of course, audience plays just as large a role in the modified proposal as it
does in the technical proposal. The audience of the general proposal, however, is
seldom asked to take specific action. Rather, the audience is encouraged to support in some general sense the actions of others.

In the article on national health care at the end of this book, try to identify the
problem and solution sections set up by Steffie Woolhandler and David U. Himmelstein. Are there any other conventions of the proposal discussed in this chapter? How detailed is their solution to the problem?

In the Proposal for the Modification of Radio Station WMTB, at the end of
this chapter, examine the organization and use of the appendix. Can you make
observations about the identity of the audience and the objections the writer
seems to anticipate?

Writing Assignments

1. Write a proposal calling for a physical change on your campus
   (better studying facilities/better library facilities).
2. Write a proposal calling for an academic change in your college.
3. Propose a course of action on one of the following issues: gun
   control, euthanasia, health care. For instance, one might consider whether euthanasia should be outlawed, restricted, or
   embraced by the public.
4. Write a letter on behalf of a charitable organization requesting
   donations or political action. Be sure to explain why the organization needs donation, or the political support, now.
5. Write an essay in which you identify a problem or series of
   problems and propose a solution for it. Here are four possible
   steps for developing the paper.
   (a) Identify the problem or problems. Use this section to
       explain the nature of the problem; tell which of the writers
       we have read so far address the problem.

(b) Discuss the seriousness of the problem. How pervasive is the problem? Is the problem limited to a certain group or class of people, or does it cut across all social and economic lines? What evidence do you have that the problem is serious?

(c) Discuss possible solutions. Is the problem solvable? How do others suggest solving the problem? What other solutions have you considered?

(d) What is the best solution? In this section you can side with a particular writer or pose your own solution. If in fact there is no single solution, it might be better to suggest that a way be found to respond to the problem rather than to "solve" it.

6. You have been hired by the provost of a medium-sized state college (3500 full-time students) as a consultant on student media. The college has a journalism program, but the school's weekly newspaper is published independently by a student organization advised by a faculty member. The paper receives its funding entirely through selling advertising, but its offices are in the student union building and its editors receive full scholarships.

You have been hired specifically to help the provost work out a policy concerning the college's relationship to the newspaper. This job has recently been complicated by the following circumstances.

Last fall the newspaper ran an ad for a gay bar in the town. Soon letters from angry parents began pouring into the provost's office asking what she was going to do about the lack of morals exhibited by the student press. A college chaplain also complained in writing, sending copies of his letter to the dean and to the board of trustees.

Two weeks later the newspaper reported that a high college official had misrepresented his graduate and military records. Although the story was essentially true, it caused great embarrassment to the administration, which had recently promoted the person.

The most recent issue contained an article accusing a member of the board of trustees of being a slum landlord; a photograph of one of these buildings showed used syringes lying on the steps near some children playing hopscotch. It soon develops, however, that the trustee, who had noticed conditions in the apartment complex deteriorating several years ago, sold his interest at that time. Now the board member threatens a lawsuit and has asked the provost to meet with the board of trustees to explain what she's going to do about the paper. Your proposal is intended to help her gather her thoughts.

The provost, as well as the board of trustees, is aware of the thrust of the *Hazelwood* decision—namely, that the protection of the First Amendment is not guaranteed to high school newspapers, which can be subject to oversight by high school administrators. The board of trustees would like to see a mechanism for administrative oversight implemented in this case. The provost is aware that the *Hazelwood* ruling does not explicitly extend beyond the high school level, but she also knows that there is considerable pressure from faculty, administration, and the board of trustees to crack down on the student paper.

What should you tell her to do?

Work Cited

Woolhandler, Steffie and David U. Himmelstein, "Socialized Medicine Is Good Business." *In These Times* 25 Jan. 1993. Rpt. in *Health Care in America: Opposing Viewpoints*. San Diego: Greenhaven, 1994. 135–41.

Proposal for the Disposition
of
Radio Station WMTB

To: Media Council
From: Ad Hoc Radio Committee
Date:

Contents

Proposal
   Introduction
   Problem
   Moving WMTB's Antenna
      Federal Communications Commission Requirements
      Site
   Other Solutions
      Carrier Current
      Closed-Circuit System
   Advantages of a 100-Watt Station
      Student Interest
      Range of Audience
      Breadth of Programming
Conclusions

Appendix
   Exhibit 1 Engineering Report from Silliman and
           Silliman
         2 Engineering Report from Fran Little
         3 Map of Projected Location
         4 Itemized Cost of Moving WMTB Antenna
            (equipment needed)
         5 Estimate Sheet for Housing of Equipment
            (James Widner, director of the physical
            plant)
         6 Total Estimated Cost for Moving WMTB
            Antenna
         7 Letter from Mike Kennedy, director of
            admissions

Introduction

On Thursday, March 31, and Thursday, April 7, students and faculty on the Ad Hoc Radio Committee met to discuss possible solutions to the problems WMTB has been experiencing and also to discuss the role of the station relative to student life and to a possible communications program. This report presents the conclusions of the committee.

Problem

Since WMTB increased its power to 100 watts, station leaders have received numerous complaints of interference. As you know, the new 100-watt antenna replaced the old 10-watt antenna on top of Dubois Hall on the hill above campus. Since then, residents of the hall have complained that they are unable to receive any stations other than WMTB.

Interference seemed to be most prevalent in FM reception in Dubois Hall, although a few students did report some interference in the apartments. Even in Dubois, however, interference was sporadic, and most students did not seem to be affected by it. Nevertheless, many students and a few faculty were inconvenienced.

According to both engineers' reports (see Exhibits 1 and 2), the interference was caused by "front end overload." This means that the interference was not a result of "spurious" radio waves but occurred when certain radio receivers were not able to filter out radio waves transmitted nearby. Both engineers found the equipment at the station to be in perfect working order, and both concluded that the only way to eliminate the problem was to move the antenna to a location sufficiently remote to eliminate most front end overload. James Kenman of Silliman and Silliman suggested a minimum of 600 feet (see Exhibit 1).

Moving WMTB's Antenna

Federal Communications Commission Requirements

According to Edward F. Perry Jr. of Educational FM Associates (consultant for the FCC), antennas may be moved a quarter-mile from their current location, the only stipulation being that FCC approval be obtained. This requires the completion of form 340, which takes 3–5 months to process. Perry added, however, that the FCC is likely to approve any move up to half a mile (although it is not obliged to do so); for moves over half a mile a terrain check is required, at a cost of approximately $1,000.

Site

The most promising site for a remote antenna would be as far from the present location as possible without exceeding the FCC limit for terrain checks. The best place seems to be a relatively flat area of land on the mountain approximately three-eighths mile from Dubois Hall and one-eighth mile above the cemetery (approximately 150 yards south of the large reservoir) (see Exhibit 3). The projected cost of such a move, including land clearing, shack, equipment, and labor, would total $8,428–$9,353 (see Exhibits 4–6).

Other Solutions

1. Carrier Current

This option was not fully explored by the committee because of initial indications that it would be both expensive and potentially troublesome. While carrier current doesn't interfere with radio reception as a rule, it does interfere with virtually everything else that runs on electrical current, including lights.

2. Closed-Circuit System

This would involve using the college's current closed-circuit TV equipment by piping in the station through one of the vacant TV channels. Although the cost would be minimal, this option would effectively shut down the station, since few students would be willing to use their TV receivers solely for audio transmissions. Also, the station would be unavailable to everyone living off campus.

Advantages of a 100-Watt Station

The Ad Hoc Radio Committee found the following to be the major advantages of remaining a 100-watt station.

1. Student Interest

Currently, the staff of WMTB consists of 60 students. In addition, three faculty members broadcast their own shows in the evenings and on weekends. It is unlikely that a closed radio system would generate the same breadth of interest found in the current station. This likelihood warrants attention particularly in light of the college's need to offer a broad range of nonathletic extracurricular activities.

Furthermore, a 100-watt station provides an important attraction for incoming freshmen and transfer students who, while not majoring in communications, wish to become active in serious broadcasting (see Exhibit 7). The station also has an important role in enhancing professional training and résumés.

As well as attracting students, the station trains students in programming techniques. Students must learn to be familiar with the genres they broadcast by studying the literature of music, attending conferences, and talking with professional programmers like David Einstein of WHFS, who visited the station last fall.

2. Range of Audience

At full 100-watt power the station can reach a radius of 50 miles and has a potential audience of over 200,000 people (124,000 in our county alone)—an area of major recruiting for the college. WMTB could be an invaluable public relations tool to introduce the college to members of the potential audience who are unfamiliar with the station but interested in our type of programming.

In addition, the station provides news and announcements of campus activities as well as play-by-play coverage of major sporting events to students, faculty, and staff who live off campus.

3. Breadth of Programming

One purpose of a college radio station is to be educational—to introduce on-campus listeners to a range of music and programming. Since the station has gone 100 watts and reaches a wider audience, it has been able to provide a range of music—jazz, rhythm and blues, traditional folk, and other programs. A closed-system station would not be likely to offer this range of programming; nor would it counteract the insularity of the students and campus.

Conclusions

The committee recommends that WMTB be maintained at 100 watts. Even though moving the antenna will not be inexpensive, it is necessary if the station is to develop to its potential in serving the college.

Professionally operated radio stations not only offer college students valuable experience in developing their communications skills, but they also serve as important promotional tools. A fully operational 100-watt station on this campus reaches an audience that includes prospective students and others who have no contact with the college other than WMTB.

Furthermore, strong, well-supported student media ought to supplement a successful communication arts program. A good newspaper and a radio station that has a public audience ought to provide the link between communication theory and practice.

CHAPTER

9

Preparing Oral Presentations

The oral presentation of arguments makes use of many of the techniques learned in writing arguments. Oral arguments require careful analysis, clear organization, and thorough attention to audience. While oral presentations tend to be a little less formal than written arguments, they offer special opportunities to practice argumentation skills.

In fact, people are far more often likely to use oral arguments than written ones. Oral presentations may be given along with a written proposal, for instance; sometimes they even replace written proposals. Sooner or later nearly everyone winds up speaking before a civic group, a town council, or a school board.

Many of the writing strategies learned in this book apply to speaking as well. This is particularly true in analyzing audiences. The preliminary questions to be asked are much the same in both cases. Speakers need to decide whether they want audiences to act, to accept different viewpoints, or to modify views presently held. Because the audience for an oral presentation can be seen, its reaction can usually be assessed rapidly. Are the people listening with rapt attention? Do they appear skeptical? Are they looking at their watches? The answers to all these questions provide clues to how the audience responds to the speaker and the speaker's message. Of course, to take advantage of this information fully, the presenter has to maintain enough flexibility to adjust to what is being observed.

And now for a caveat. There's nothing disgraceful about bombing a speech or boring an audience. Everyone does it. Anyone who has given more than a few presentations knows that sometimes speakers misread their audiences—or misread the audience interest level in their topic. That's perfectly all right—as long as the speaker acts quickly to redress the situation. The real problem comes when a speaker fails to make adjustments to an audience. I once witnessed a speaker use thirty transparencies in a half-hour presentation. Worse, he used them badly— he placed one after another on the overhead projector and read aloud what everyone else could see. The audience justifiably grew irritated. Some pulled out newspapers; some talked among themselves; a few walked out. But the speaker seemed oblivious to the problem. Instead of saying, "I brought all these transparencies, but why don't I just summarize them for you," he continued on and on, robotlike, to the bitter end. A speaker can take advantage of what is learned from the audience only if he or she is willing to make adjustments in midstream.

The strong connection between audience and speaker in oral arguments provides the speaker with valuable information in constructing an oral presentation. It will likely be easier to evaluate and analyze issues if the audience is well defined. If the audience comprises students and faculty at one's own institution, it should be possible to gauge their knowledge of, attitudes about, and interest level in a given topic.

Finally, considering persona is as valuable for oral presentations as for written ones. Does the speaker mean to be angry or conciliatory? How strongly does he or she believe in the position set forth? What is the purpose of the presentation? (Must the audience come completely around to the speaker's position, or will intent to rethink the issue be satisfactory?) The persona of a speaker addressing a group is at least as striking as that of a writer. Not only does the audience listen to the spoken words, they observe what kind of clothes the speaker is wearing; they note hairstyle, how frequently one consults notes, and posture (straight and relaxed, straight and tense, or slouched).

Strategies for Oral Presentations

It's safe to say that all speakers experience some degree of nervousness at just the thought of presenting an argument before a class (or speaking on any subject to any group). Studies have shown that many people fear public speaking only slightly less than death. The skills of good public speaking are not mysterious, however. They can be taught and learned. More than anything, they need to be practiced. Here are some things to keep in mind in preparing to speak before a group.

Voice Control and Projection

When people get nervous, the muscles in their necks contract, closing off the orifice most needed during the act of speech. Matters are made worse if the speaker tightens the shoulders and hangs on to a podium for dear life. The result is often a soft, squeaky voice that lacks much of its normal power. There are several ways to work on voice control.

First, find ways to reduce the tension in the rest of the body. Work on relaxing the shoulder and neck muscles in particular. There are many exercises designed to help do this (e.g., head rolls, arm stretches). The exercises may be done immediately before a speech (unless one is just finishing the chicken dinner).

Second, speak from the diaphragm, not the throat. The diaphragm is the muscle beneath the stomach that helps control the amount of air flowing into the lungs. Wind musicians know that when they breathe from the diaphragm, the instrument will sound deeper and richer. The same is true for the voice.

Body Movement and Gestures

Good speakers know how to use the whole body effectively in presentations. The physical presence of a speaker is as important to the oral message as the tone is to the written one. Developing a relaxed and natural physical delivery takes some time and practice.

Be conscious of what is done with the arms. For speakers who are really nervous, especially during the first few tries at public speaking, the podium can be used as a security blanket. Holding on to it may not be as effective as using arms for gestures, but it's much better than keeping hands in pockets, folded across the chest, or gripped behind the back. As speakers become more at ease with delivering a speech, they can work on freeing themselves from the podium by giving carefully planned arm and hand gestures. Gestures ought to be visible, not low, near or below podium level, and they should serve a purpose.

Equally important, be conscious of leg movement. Many speakers sway as they speak, move from leg to leg, or lock their knees during presentations. Speakers ought to stand firmly and comfortably in front of a group, whether behind a podium or without one. As speakers develop expertise, they become more able to break free from the podium, moving toward or around the audience. This is a difficult step, however, and it won't necessarily be accomplished without some apprehension.

Speakers make contact with their audience in a number of ways. Besides the physical act of leaving the podium, eye contact provides the best way to connect with the audience. Looking directly at people is a powerful way to keep their attention. How many times have you had someone you had been watching covertly turn around and look you directly in the eye as though aware of your attention? As a motorcycle rider I know the importance of eye contact at intersections, even if I'm wearing a helmet and sunglasses.

Eye contact is very powerful, and it can be used to advantage in oral presentations. Look at the audience. See if their response to the presentation can be gauged. The best speakers use frequent eye contact even when they're addressing large groups.

Of course, there are pitfalls to making contact with an audience as well. As people first begin speaking before audiences, they're usually unaware of all the mannerisms they have that distract an audience from a message. This is natural. Speakers may not realize that they tend to run their fingers through their hair when they're nervous, put their hands in their pockets, stand on one leg, or punctuate each phrase with "ah" or "you know."

First, it's necessary to identify the kinds of involuntary gesture that need to be eliminated. The best way to do this is to watch a videotape of oneself. But friends, classmates, and instructors can also be called on for help. Second, do something about the problems that have been identified. And that leads to the next tip: practice.

Using Notes in Oral Presentations

There are several methods for preparing a text to be used for speaking in front of groups. One of the most hazardous ways (and one of the most difficult to do well) is to read from a prepared text. Think about the last time you watched someone read a prepared text. In all likelihood the experience was not pleasant. People tend to use prepared texts when they're afraid they will forget what they have to say; but listening to someone read a paper can be dreadfully dull. Often the speaker makes little use of eye contact, reading to the paper instead of to the audience. When eye contact is used, however, the speaker must be careful to keep place in the text. Oral interpretation (which is what reading a prepared text is called) is a very difficult performance medium. It requires both an intimate knowledge of the text (enough to maintain extensive eye contact with the audience) and an ability to use voice inflection and eye contact in effective ways.

A much better approach is to talk from notes. The notes can be detailed or abbreviated, depending on the speaker's confidence and memory. The speaker who uses notes doesn't need to be quite as concerned about getting lost, and carefully constructed headings can prevent this disaster almost completely.

Sometimes one is forced to speak extemporaneously—that is, without text or notes, and perhaps with only a limited time to prepare. Extemporaneous speeches happen by design during debate cross-examinations when speakers have seconds to respond. Speakers also respond extemporaneously during question-and-answer sessions at the end of talks or in filling in for a master of ceremonies who suddenly develops laryngitis. The poise needed for these situations will come with practice.

Of course, speakers may choose to use any combination of methods. Some of the most effective presentations I have heard have come from people who brought notes and never referred to them. These speakers knew what they wanted to say and had the confidence to say it well. They may have *needed* the notes to help put them at ease, however. Knowing the notes will bail them out if necessary gives the speakers the confidence to talk without using them.

Practice

The best way to be certain that notes will be adequate, gestures effective, and the voice well modulated is to practice. Perhaps the best way to practice is in front of a video camera, if one is available. Although speaking in front of a camera can be unnerving at first, soon one forgets that the equipment is there. Watching oneself on tape is an excellent way to improve presentations.

Videotaping is not the only way to practice, however. I frequently like to rehearse my presentations alone at home. Working with only oneself for an audience will help identify rough spots in the notes or in the preparation. Other good techniques include speaking in front of a mirror or in front of a friend or roommate. The best speakers practice over and over, with the result that when they finally face an audience, they have the presence of mind to concentrate not just on the text but on movement, gestures, and voice modulation.

A Short Course on Debate

One way to put the skills of oral argument to immediate use is through debate. Based on legislative and judicial argument, debate formalizes the presentation of opposing sides. A debating team usually comprises two to six members, each presenting arguments or rebutting the arguments of others.

In one sense, the philosophy of debate seems to be at odds with the philosophy of argument as discovery of issues. Debate, after all, is based on winning and losing. When one side presents a "point," the other side tries to refute that point. Seen from this vantage, debate has more in common with boxing than with inquiry. Even in formal presidential debates, the news media are quick to announce "winners" and "losers."

In many ways debate and other forms of argument make very different uses of audience. Participants are not expected to change or even modify their beliefs as a result of the debate itself. The audience witnesses the exchange of ideas but does not participate, and even when it plays a role in judging, the criteria do not reflect the audience's stance but serve to indicate whether the teams have adequately put forth and defended their positions.

However, the larger purpose of debate is to generate an understanding of the whole issue being analyzed. Debate fleshes out the many positions that can be taken on an issue. It's an attempt to say, "Here, you take this stance and see how well it fares against this other stance." It's a game in which the participants temporarily put aside their own viewpoints to explore an issue; and seen as a game, it provides valuable training in bouncing one issue off another. Debates require that participants become familiar with multiple sides of issues to be able to refute opposing teams more effectively and to argue other sides in subsequent debates, if necessary.

The Mechanics of a Debate

There are several ways to structure a debate. The "Oxford" or "standard" model pits two teams of two members each in the following order:

First affirmative	10 minutes
First negative	10 minutes
Second affirmative	10 minutes
Second negative	10 minutes
First negative	5 minutes
First affirmative	5 minutes
Second negative	5 minutes
Second affirmative	5 minutes

While the time limits for the speakers can be modified to suit the occasion, the basic principle of the debate does not change.

The affirmative team is responsible for formulating a position called a thesis statement, which is articulated by the first affirmative speaker and developed by the second affirmative speaker. This thesis is known as a *problem statement*. The problem statement must be carefully articulated before the debate and carefully developed during the contest, especially through the first two affirmative speeches. The affirmative team is responsible not just for defending this thesis but for explaining what it means and defining each key term.

Usually, the problem statement proposes a *change to the status quo*. The affirmative team argues for a change in a current policy, usually by showing why a problem exists in the current state of affairs and why and how the affirmative proposition will respond to the problem. If this sounds like the psychology of a proposal, it should. Debates have much in common with proposal writing. The negative team argues that change in the status quo is neither needed nor desirable and shows how a change would be ineffective at best and at worst would create new problems. Points in debate are awarded for positions clearly stated, for the quality of support for these positions, and, to a lesser extent, for skill shown in delivery.

There are other kinds of debate as well. In the "cross-examination" model each side has the opportunity to directly question the members of the other team. This somewhat more sophisticated format forces participants to engage in extemporaneous public discussion and in actively questioning the other participants. During the break period, teams confer to help the cross-examiner develop a response to the opposing team. The order for cross-examination usually looks like this:

First affirmative	8 minutes
Break	3 minutes
Negative cross-examination of first affirmative	3 minutes
First negative	8 minutes
Break	3 minutes
Affirmative cross-examination of first negative	3 minutes
Second affirmative	8 minutes
Break	3 minutes
Negative cross-examination of second affirmative	3 minutes
Second negative	8 minutes
Break	3 minutes
Affirmative cross-examination of second negative	3 minutes

In the third type of debate, the "Lincoln-Douglas" model, there is only one member per team. Based on the famous debate between Abraham Lincoln and Stephen Douglas during the 1852 senate race in Illinois, this model requires participants to argue and to cross-examine each other over questions of value. Here is the typical format for a Lincoln-Douglas debate:

Affirmative	6 minutes
Cross-examination by negative	3 minutes
Negative	7 minutes
Cross-examination by affirmative	3 minutes
Affirmative rebuttal	4 minutes
Negative rebuttal	6 minutes
Affirmative rebuttal	3 minutes

The time limits on all types of debate can be modified to fit the situation. Also, the models can be combined in various ways. It is possible, for instance, to hold a modified standard debate in which each participant is cross-examined by a member of the other team. In the cross-examination model, participants may actively ask questions of the opposing speakers, usually for a short period. Participants should direct their questions as much as possible to assertions developed in the presentations of the speaker being questioned, but they might also stray into assertions developed by other members of the opposing team.

Those speaking later in a debate often have less time for their presentations than those speaking early, largely because the final speakers are responding to topics already introduced, not announcing new topics. The last few negative speakers, for instance, must listen carefully to their affirmative counterparts and respond directly to the affirmative's assertions. The last few affirmative speakers are obliged to listen closely to the assertions made by the negative team and counter them.

To do their jobs, team members need to take careful notes when the other team speaks. Taking notes while the speeches are in progress is known as *flowing* the debate. Flowing well is important because it helps enable one to respond to arguments in a timely manner. It does little good to come up with a brilliant response five minutes after the final rebuttal. Taking good notes is very helpful in learning to become clear and effective as a speaker.

Debaters need to identify accurately the central points used by the opposition and state their refutations in ways that clearly address these points. Debates are scored on the ability of each speaker to refute points brought up by the opposition. That means that teams must be very careful in defining those points precisely for the judge, and in indicating clearly how each point is being refuted.

A number of fine books set forth the strategies of debate in much greater detail than has been possible here. Three useful references are Fryar, Thomas, and Goodnight's *Basic Debate*, Wood and Goodnight's *Strategic Debate*, and Freeley's *Argumentation and Debate*.

Classroom Activities

Exercise 1

Arrange a debate (or series of debates) around an issue addressed in one of the writing assignments for this class. Teams may have two, three, or five members. Here are some possible pairings:

For two people per side:

First affirmative	5 minutes
First negative	5 minutes
Second negative	5 minutes
Second affirmative	5 minutes

For three people per side:

First affirmative	5 minutes
First negative	5 minutes
Second affirmative	5 minutes
Second negative	5 minutes
Third negative	3 minutes
Third affirmative	3 minutes

Also for three people per side:

First affirmative	5 minutes
Break	2.5 minutes
Negative cross-examination	3 minutes
First negative	5 minutes
Break	2.5 minutes
Affirmative cross-examination	3 minutes
Second affirmative	5 minutes
Break	2.5 minutes
Negative cross-examination	3 minutes
Second negative	5 minutes
Break	2.5 minutes
Affirmative cross-examination	3 minutes

N.B. In this model one person gives both affirmative cross-examinations and another person gives both negative cross-examinations.

Judging the Debate

Before selecting someone to judge the debate, establish the criteria on which the debate will be decided. Weights should be assigned to such factors as depth of analysis, persuasiveness of the assertions, support for assertions, quality of rebuttals, and quality of delivery. Here are some possible ways to have the debate judged.

1. Pass out ballots listing the criteria and have the class rate the teams on each criterion. The ballots can then be tabulated on the basis of the scores.
2. Have the teacher judge.
3. Bring in a guest judge (ideally, an experienced debate judge).

Exercise 2

Arrange a series of Lincoln-Douglas debates. Divide students into pairs of debaters. Here is one possible model:

Affirmative	3 minutes
Negative	5 minutes
Affirmative	2 minutes

The time limits on these debates can be lengthened or shortened as long as the negative and affirmative end up with the same number of minutes. Either format may also be combined with the cross-examination method to provide a model that looks something like this:

Affirmative	3 minutes
Cross-examination by negative	2 minutes
Negative	5 minutes
Cross-examination by affirmative	2 minutes
Affirmative	2 minutes

Exercise 3

Arrange a series of individual speeches based on topics developed earlier in the semester. The presentations ought to have specific time limits (e.g., 5–7 minutes). It's advisable not to permit the reading of speeches, even if the material initially was prepared as part of a written assignment.

Works Cited

Freeley, Austin J. *Argumentation and Debate: Reasoned Decision Making*. 5th ed. Belmont, CA: Wadsworth, 1981.

Fryar, Maridell, David A. Thomas, and Lynn Goodnight. *Basic Debate*. 3rd ed. Lincolnwood, IL: National Textbook, 1989.

Wood, Roy V. and Lynn Goodnight. *Strategic Debate*. 4th ed. Lincolnwood, IL: National Textbook, 1989.

10

Conclusion

This book has explored a number of methods of argument and a number of ways to make arguments sharp and effective. Stasis theory and the models of Toulmin and Rogers all provide helpful starting points for argument. All these in some way address the intersecting demands of reader, writer (or speaker), and message. Each one, however, focuses on a different aspect of this context.

It's important to recognize that no one technique will work equally well for everyone. Toulmin's theory of argument and Carl Rogers's model from psychology approach the nature of argument from different vantage points The Rogerian focus on the audience and on the relationship between arguers and listeners will likely be very effective for people who are good at negotiation, for those who want to practice skills in negotiation, and for those who need to function in highly emotional or controversial contexts. In fact, for Rogers the relationship between arguer and audience becomes symbiotic: each depends on the other for support, and each, in turn, can be influenced and changed by the other. Rogers's method will be particularly useful for writers who are concerned with developing an ear for the tone of their arguments and determining the likely effect of their words on an audience.

Toulmin's model of argument focuses much more on the structure of the argument than on the more narrow writer-audience relationship. While Toulmin acknowledges that all argument takes place in a context of reader, writer, and method, his system demands a clear representation of ideas, starting with an articulate statement of a claim and the development of adequate data to support the claim. Toulmin's system will encourage writers to look carefully at the terms they use and to be conscious of the relationship between claims and support. Toulmin's model is conceptual, while Rogers's is interpersonal.

Stasis theory is probably the most versatile of the three systems. We have already seen how stasis theory is adaptable to the courtroom and how it has been used for over two millennia as a technique to teach courtroom argumentation. It's equally at home in civil deliberation, in the courthouse, in legislative halls, and in any other place that values the sharp exchange of ideas on controversial issues. As a tool for antagonistic argument, stasis can assist one in identifying central points of contention between arguer and audience. In this sense it is a conceptual system not unlike Toulmin's.

The value of stasis is not limited to arguing positions. It can also be used in analyzing issues, in troubleshooting problems, and in finding creative solutions to them. It can even be used to address interpersonal conflict. Someone who is experiencing difficulties in a relationship with a friend may do well to stop and ask, "What kind(s) of problem are we having? Are the problems personality conflicts (she's an extrovert; I'm an introvert), habit (she leaves her clothes all over the room; I'm a neat-freak), or cultural (she's not used to our customs)?" Even if the problems cover more than one category, stasis theory provides a way to identify problems, categorize them, and work toward solving them.

Although this book has focused primarily on deliberative arguments requiring careful analysis and preparation, the methods introduced can be equally valuable in responding to arguments faced in day-to-day situations. In practice one does not always have time for careful deliberation. Arguments often take place in informal settings where the conversation is spontaneous. People may be challenged in the classroom by teachers and by students, at the dinner table by family members, or at their doorsteps by religious devotees. The methods developed in this book can be useful in these spontaneous situations. In fact, the methods implied in the enthymeme, stasis, Toulmin, and Rogers approaches can be very useful in knowing how to respond when there's no time for library research. Here are a few ways these models can help.

Look for *hidden assumptions* in the arguments of others. People frequently use arguments with hidden premises and assumptions. When someone says, "Fredonia is an evil country because it is socialist," think about the statement as an *enthymeme*, and ask "What is the hidden premise?" In this case it is "All socialist countries are evil." The syllogism would look like this:

All socialist countries are evil. (major premise)
Fredonia is a socialist country. (minor premise)
Fredonia is evil. (conclusion)

One can respond to such an argument by questioning either the minor premise (Is Fredonia, in fact, a socialist country?) or the major premise (Can the assertion that "all socialist countries are evil" be defended?). The person can be asked whether there aren't examples of socialist countries that are not evil.

Look for *qualifications* that may make the claim invalid. This kind of reasoning may draw specifically on Stephen Toulmin's model. One can counter the assertion "All lies are immoral" by questioning whether the statement may not sometimes be open to qualification. What if one tells a lie to save a life or to avoid disastrous consequences to the public at large?

Similarly, opponents can be asked to *define key terms*. Someone who asserts that "all crimes are immoral" can be asked to define "crime." Is it a crime to disregard *any* law imposed by the state? If so, is it possible for the laws themselves, not the disregard of them, to be immoral? How would one evaluate the residents of the French village of Le Chambon who saved thousands of Jews from death at the hands of the Nazis? The Nazi persecution of Jews was technically "legal" while the protective action of the French villagers was "illegal." In the argument over the nature of Fredonia, one could ask for a clear definition of "socialist." Is the term defined in a way (like "undemocratic") that would also permit theocracies to be considered socialist? If so, one could point out the apparent contradiction in calling all theocracies "evil."

Remembering the terms of stasis, one might also make sure that opponents have taken into consideration all the appropriate *categories* of argument. Someone who says "Prayer in public schools is a moral issue" might be asked whether the matter doesn't also entail church-state relations, the law, and/or civil rights. In other words, the field of the argument can be widened and the force of the narrower argument weakened.

It will also be useful to examine the *quality of support* carefully. This approach can be particularly effective when someone produces suspicious evidence or data that are not familiar to the arguer. A person who documents the assertion that UFOs brought human life to this planet with reference to a book just published in Britain should be challenged to produce the book or to demonstrate in detail the quality of the unavailable evidence. If the book is produced, look at the Works Cited section. Are the author's sources scholarly journals of anthropology or archaeology or tabloids?

Finally, if one is engaged in a highly emotional argument, say one involving abortion or gay rights, remember Carl Rogers and try to *modify the purpose* of the argument. For instance, one could point out that the competing positions in the argument about abortion are irreconcilable and that no resolution is possible if the arguers can't agree on the existence of a woman's right to choose or a fetus's right to be born. The argument may not be won or lost, but at least there's a chance of putting it to rest without bloodshed.

These suggestions are not exhaustive, but they will aid in identifying quickly the weak points of arguments and suggesting strategies to respond to them.

Just as people have different styles of argument, they have different styles of invention and composition. Those who have a pronounced visual orientation may use mapping as a way to chart out issues. Others may find strategies like freewriting more valuable. Some will benefit more by using arguments orally, through debate, informal discussion, and formal reports; still others will respond to the strategies of Stephen Toulmin or Carl Rogers. It's important that a writer find the strategy or strategies that work best for himself or herself.

Finally, problem solving and argumentation require practice. This book supplies the principles of good argument, but you have to hone them yourself. Take every opportunity to speak in front of groups and to write arguments. There are many forums for your argumentative skills. Write letters to the editor, opinion pieces, and commentary. Take issues of concern to you before the student council. Through practice you will gain the experience and develop the confidence to persuade people because you have a grasp of the issues, know their concerns, and can explain your own positions articulately.

Appendix of
Chapter Readings

Table of Contents

CHAPTER

Pesticides Must Be More Closely Regulated

by Laura Weiss

Pesticide and chemical fertilizer use go hand-in-hand with modern farming techniques. Only recently have the long-term effects of some of these chemical compounds become known. A few cancer-causing pesticides, like DDT, have been banned, but most environmental organizations would like to add many more chemicals to the outlawed list. In the following viewpoint, Laura Weiss writes that the Environmental Protection Agency (EPA) has been slow in banning many harmful pesticides. Weiss, a field organizer for the special-interest group Citizen's Watch, argues that numerous cancer-causing agents need to be taken off the agricultural market.

As you read, consider the following questions:

1. Under what conditions does Weiss believe a hazardous substance can continue to be used?
2. In the author's opinion, what happens to the 2.6 billion pounds of pesticides that are used in the U.S. each year?
3. Why does Weiss consider the use of certain pesticides particularly dangerous for farm workers?

If you're like most health-conscious Americans, you pay attention to the amount of cholesterol in your diet. But when was the last time you tried to calculate the amount of captan you've eaten?

Chances are you've never even heard of captan, let alone had any idea you might be ingesting it. You won't find it listed as an ingredient of anything you buy.

Captan is a chemical pesticide, first introduced in 1951, used to control fungus. The government permits its use on 65 different types of food crops, from apples and almonds to peaches and strawberries, even though it has classified captan as a "probable human carcinogen."

In 1980, the National Cancer Institute found that captan caused tumors in mice. Based on this and subsequent scientific data indicating that captan also caused genetic mutations, the Environmental Protection Agency (EPA) decided that the chemical warranted closer scrutiny to determine whether it should be banned from use.

So later that year EPA placed captan in a special program designed to speed the process for deciding whether to restrict or prohibit the use of potentially harmful pesticides. The program, called Special Review, was intended to enable EPA to issue a decision within 18 months.

After five years of review, in 1985 EPA proposed to prohibit all uses of captan on food crops unless its manufacturers could prove that the residues remaining on food were lower than EPA had estimated or that alternative application methods could reduce the levels. Two-and-a-half years later—and more than seven years after EPA first put captan into Special Review—the agency has yet to issue a final decision. . . .

Economics vs. Health

When EPA concludes its review, it won't necessarily either declare captan safe or order its removal from the market. Under the Federal Insecticide, Fungicide and Rodenticide Act (FIFRA), EPA is required to balance the health and environmental risks of a pesticide's use against the economic benefits. This burden is placed on the agency even though chemical manufacturers are not required to provide evidence showing that their pesticide products are effective.

Even where a pesticide is found to be hazardous to human health, wildlife, or the environment, its continued use can be permitted if EPA is persuaded that there are advantages more significant than the risks. This system places heavy emphasis on economics rather than health. As EPA economists were quoted in a 1985 World Resources Institute report, "While pesticide producers, users, and consumers benefit from the use of pesticides, . . . costs are distributed disproportionately throughout the population (in terms of acute and chronic toxic effects such as cancer).". . .

Agents of Destruction

A pesticide is, by definition, an agent of destruction: designed to kill bugs, weeds, rodents, worms, funguses, and mold. Pesticides also have some special applications, such as to sterilize medical equipment or to regulate crop growth. Nearly 80 percent of all pesticides are used in agriculture; the rest are used for industrial and consumer purposes.

Today, more than 2.6 *billion* pounds of pesticides are used annually in the United States. Long after they have served their intended purpose they can persist in the environment, seeping into groundwater, contaminating food supplies, and accumulating in the tissue of plants, animals, and people. They are capable of causing birth defects, genetic mutations, sterility, and cancer.

Many environmentalists, scientists, and farmers are convinced that we have become overdependent on pesticides. Conventional farming interests such as the Farm Bureau argue that large-scale food production is not possible without pesticides and that consumers need these chemicals to control germs, pests, and weeds. But a growing movement toward non-chemical pest control belies these claims. The U.S. Department of Agriculture estimates that 30,000 farmers are now raising crops without chemicals or are close to eliminating their use, and other experts say the numbers range from 50,000 to 100,000.

Under the federal law, originally enacted in 1947, all pesticides must be licensed, or "registered," by the government before they may be sold. The law was originally enacted to ensure that pesticide products performed as claimed; later amendments gave EPA responsibility for monitoring pesticides' health and environmental risks.

As amended, FIFRA requires a company seeking to register a pesticide to submit scientific data on the chemical's health and environmental effects. However, many pesticides have been registered without complete supporting data, or were registered prior to current scientific knowledge of their potentially adverse effects. The National Academy of Sciences estimated in 1984 that 90 percent of the registered pesticides had not been adequately tested for their health and environmental effects.

Because so many of the registration records are incomplete, in 1972 Congress directed EPA to "reregister" some 600 active ingredients that are used in about 50,000 pesticide products. Since then the agency has moved at a snail's pace in its reregistration program despite public concern about the dangers of many of the pesticides. Since 1972, the agency has reregistered only 17 active ingredients. In the course of its reexamination process, however, EPA has identified a number of pesticides that pose the greatest risks to human health or the environment; these are the ones that have been placed in Special Review.

As of 1988, 17 reviews (involving 34 active ingredients) have been ongoing for an average of about four years; for many of these, EPA is years away from issuing a final regulatory decision. Another 33 Special Reviews (involving 53 ingredients) that have ended have taken an average of about four years before either EPA issued a decision, or the manufacturer voluntarily withdrew the product from the market. EPA may continue to gather and examine data on a pesticide under the reregistration process even after a Special Review has ended, which is why many of the pesticides that have completed Special Review are still not reregistered.

"Acceptable" Cancer Levels

One of the reasons Special Reviews take longer than was originally intended is that much of the data necessary to determine the safety of a pesticide is missing and must be collected. The soil fumigant 1,3-dichloropropene (1,3-D) was registered more than two decades ago. Although the chemical was licensed for use on food crops, the manufacturer was never required to submit data showing whether or not residues remained on food until 1986, when the chemical was placed in Special Review because tests showed it caused cancer in lab animals. No action will be taken on 1,3-D until Dow Chemical Co. submits new data. In the meantime, Dow can continue to market the fumigant.

If, based on available data, EPA concludes that risks can be held to an "acceptable" level—by reducing food residue levels or imposing use restrictions, for example—then it will uphold the pesticide's registration. In evaluating cancer risk, for example, EPA has defined "acceptable" to mean that the pesticide is not likely to cause more than "one additional case of cancer in the lifetime of 1 million persons." However, EPA can be persuaded to approve a pesticide that poses a greater than acceptable risk if its manufacturers and users contend that there is no adequate substitute, that the pesticide is uniquely suitable for particular applications, or that there are other benefits from continued use.

EPA may decide to cancel some uses of a pesticide because of unacceptably high risks, but permit other uses to continue. In October 1986, after only 10 months of Special Review deliberation, EPA issued a final decision to prohibit the use of diazinon on golf courses and sod farms based on evidence that the chemical had killed birds from 23 different species. Diazinon is apparently so toxic to birds that large numbers have fallen dead on the greens soon after coming into contact with the chemical.

Dangerous Alternatives

Common sense would suggest that if diazinon kills birds when it is sprayed on golf courses, it kills birds when sprayed on apple orchards or corn fields. But EPA has not proposed to cancel any of the food crop uses of the chemical because, as

Jay Ellenberger, chief of the Regulatory Management Section of EPA's Special Review Branch, explains, without the "smoking gun" of bird carcasses from diazinon-sprayed crop fields, the agency probably couldn't uphold its case on appeal. Apparently EPA does not have any such evidence nor the resources to get it. Meanwhile, diazinon manufacturers are appealing EPA's partial ban.

As part of its risk/benefit analysis, EPA considers the alternatives available. However, the alternatives to a dangerous chemical may be no less hazardous. Three of the five effective chemical replacements for benomyl, a potentially hazardous fungicide evaluated under Special Review, are or have also been in Special Review. Non-chemical alternatives receive only minor consideration by EPA, even though many farmers are moving away from chemical-based agricultural techniques. The agency only has five staff members devoted to non-chemical pest control methods, and as a result the Special Review staff receives limited information about non-chemical alternatives.

Another flaw in EPA's risk/benefit analyses is that the agency does not have to evaluate whether the pesticide under review is effective and provides the benefits intended. This is because a 1978 amendment, successfully sought by agribusiness interests, permits EPA to waive that data requirement.

Farm Workers

In many cases, farm workers who apply pesticides, work in sprayed fields, and handle freshly sprayed crops face much greater exposure risks than does the general population. The Occupational Safety and Health Administration does not have jurisdiction over farm worker exposure to pesticides; however, EPA may impose "use restrictions" intended to protect workers. For example, EPA may require that workers wear protective clothing when applying a type of chemical, that no one be permitted to enter a sprayed area within a certain time period, or that the manufacturer print warnings and instructions for safe use on the pesticide container labels.

In a 1982 reversal of a preliminary decision to cancel the carcinogenic herbicide diallate, EPA concluded that the risk to applicators did "not appear to be unreasonable, given the benefits" of continued diallate use as long as specific use restrictions are imposed: that applicators wear protective clothing and only certified applicators use the product. Five years earlier, EPA had recommended cancelling diallate because of the cancer risk to workers who mix or apply the compound. Several scientific studies had shown that the herbicide caused tumors and gene mutations in lab animals, and might affect the nervous system.

EPA's reversal was based on new data submitted by diallate's manufacturer, Monsanto, and on the agency's finding that cancellation of diallate would cost the sugar beet industry (which consumes 60 percent of the diallate used in the U.S.) $4 million of its $500 million annual income.

It is a disputed point whether the new use restrictions for diallate will protect farm workers from the pesticide's hazards. All too frequently, says Cesar Chavez, president of the United Farm Workers Union, use restrictions are not enforced, are deliberately sidestepped by farm management, or are disregarded by farm workers ignorant of the risks. Chavez adds that label requirements are generally ineffective because "the majority of farm workers either do not speak English or they can't understand the instructions on the label because it's too technical.". . . .

Protecting Profits

"A bill that started out decades ago to protect farmers against ineffective pesticides now protects little other than the profits of the pesticide manufacturers," notes Laura Rhodes, staff attorney with Congress Watch. "The health and environmental problems caused by dangerous pesticides are insidious and slow-building. They are not as visible as automobile or industrial accidents caused by corporate negligence, but they are just as harmful.

"We cannot permit the 'silent' deaths and devastation to continue," Rhodes adds. FIFRA reforms sought by Public Citizen would repair many of the failures in the Special Review process as well as in other aspects of federal pesticide law.

Pesticides Need Not Be More Closely Regulated

by Bert L. Bohmont

Bert L. Bohmont is a professor and coordinator of pesticide programs in the college of agricultural sciences at Colorado State University in Fort Collins. In the following viewpoint, Bohmont writes that pesticides are essential for modern agricultural production. He notes that the benefits of pesticide use in producing more abundant, blemish-free crops outweigh the hazards that might be posed to humans. Bohmont argues that environmentalists, ignorant of the facts, have exaggerated the dangers of pesticide use.

As you read, consider the following questions:

1. Why does Bohmont say that pesticides are responsible for the well-being of American consumers?
2. In the author's opinion, how does public demand for unblemished produce affect pesticide use?
3. According to Bohmont, why is the actual amount of pesticides released into the atmosphere so small?

History records that agricultural chemicals have been used since ancient times; the ancient Romans are known to have used burning sulfur to control insects. They were also known to have used salt to keep the weeds under control. The ninth-century Chinese used arsenic mixed with water to control insects. Early in the 1800s, pyrethrin and rotenone were discovered to be useful as insecticides for the control of many different insect species. Paris green, a mixture of copper and arsenic, was discovered in 1865 and subsequently used to control the Colorado potato beetle. In 1882, a fungicide known as Bordeaux mixture, made from a mixture of lime and copper sulfate, was discovered to be useful as a fungicide for the control of downy mildew in grapes. Mercury dust was developed in 1890 as a seed treatment, and subsequently, in 1915, liquid mercury was developed as a seed treatment to protect seeds from fungus diseases.

The first synthetic, organic insecticides and herbicides were discovered and produced in the early 1900s; this production of synthetic pesticides preceded the subsequent discovery and production of hundreds of synthetic, organic pesticides, starting in the 1940s. Chlorinated hydrocarbons came into commercial production in the 1940s, and organic phosphates began to be commercially produced during the 1950s. In the late 1950s, carbamates were developed and included insecticides, herbicides, and fungicides. The 1960s saw a trend toward specific and specialized pesticides, which included systemic materials and the trend toward "prescription" types of pesticides. Many of these new families of pesticides are so biologically active that they are applied at rates of grams or ounces per acre. These include the pyrethroids, sulfonylureas, and imidazolinones. Most of the newer compounds offer greater safety to the user and the environment. Presently, there are over 600 active pesticide chemicals being formulated into over 30,000 commercial preparations. Approximately 200 of the 600 basic active chemicals represent 90% of the agricultural uses in the United States.

Improving Human Life

Pesticides are used by people as intentional applications to the environment to improve environmental quality for humans, domesticated animals, and plants. Despite the fears and real problems they create, pesticides clearly are responsible for part of the physical well-being enjoyed by most people in the United States and the western world. They also contribute significantly to the existing standards of living in other nations. In the United States, consumers spend less of their income on food (about 12%) than other people anywhere. The chief reason is more efficient food production, and chemicals have made an important contribution in this area. In 1850, each U.S. farmer produced enough food and fiber for himself and three other persons; over 100 years later (1960) he was able to produce enough food and fiber for himself and 24 other people; himself and 45 other people in 1970; and in 1990 he is able to produce enough for himself and 78 other people. World population was estimated at 4.25 billion people in 1980 and is expected to increase to over 5 billion by 1990 and to over 6 billion people by the year 2000. There will be great pressure on the farmers of the world to increase agricultural production to feed and clothe this extra population.

World food supply is inadequate to satisfy the hunger of the total population. As much as one-half of the world's population is undernourished. The situation is worse in underdeveloped countries where it is estimated that as much as three-fourths of the inhabitants are undernourished.

In spite of pest control programs, U.S. agriculture still loses possibly one-third of its potential crop production to various pests. Without modern pest control, including the use of pesticides, this annual loss in the United States would probably double. If that happened, it is possible that (1) farm costs and prices would increase considerably, (2) the average consumer family would spend much more on food, (3) the number of people who work on farms would have to be increased, (4) farm exports would be reduced, and (5) a vast increase in intensive cultivated acreage would be required. It has been estimated that 418 million less acres are required to grow food and fiber than might otherwise be required. This is said to be due to modern technology, which includes the use of pesticides.

Pests and People

In most parts of the world today, pest control of some kind is essential because crops, livestock, and people live, as always, in a potentially hostile environment. Pests compete for our food supply, and they can be disease carriers as well as nuisances. Humans coexist with more than 1 million kinds of insects and other arthropods, many of which are pests. Fungi cause more than 1500 plant diseases, and there are more than 1000 species of harmful nematodes. Humans must also combat hundreds of weed species in order to grow the crops that are needed to feed our nation. Rodents and other vertebrate pests can also cause problems of major proportion. Many of these pest-enemies of humans have caused damage for centuries. . . .

Some good examples of specific increases in yields resulting from the use of pesticides in the United States are corn, 25%; potatoes, 35%; onions, 140%; cotton, 100%; alfalfa seed, 160%; and milk production, 15%.

Modern farm technology has created artificial environments that can worsen some pest problems and cause others. Large acreages, planted efficiently and economically with a single crop (monoculture), encourage certain insects and plant diseases. Advanced food production technology, therefore, actually increases the need for pest control. Pesticides are used not only to produce more food, but also food that is virtually free of damage from insects, diseases, and weeds. In the United States, pesticides are often used because of public demand, supported by government regulations, for uncontaminated and unblemished food.

Environmental Concerns

In the past, pest problems have often been solved without fully appreciating the treatments and effects on other plants and animals or on the environment. Some of these effects have been unfortunate. Today, scientists almost unanimously agree that the first rule in pest control is to recognize the whole problem.

The agricultural environment is a complex web of interactions involving (1) many kinds of pests; (2) relationships between pests and their natural enemies; (3) relationships among all these and other factors, such as weather, soil, water, plant varieties, cultural practices, wildlife, and people.

Pesticides are designed simply to destroy pests. They are applied to an environment that includes pests, crops, people, and other living things, as well as air, soil, and water. It is generally accepted that pesticides that are specific to the pest to be controlled are very desirable, and some are available. However, these products can be very expensive because of their limited range of applications.

Unquestionably, pesticides will continue to be of enormous benefit to humans. They have helped to produce food and protect health. Synthetic chemicals have been the front line of defense against destructive insects, weeds, plant diseases, and rodents. Through pest control, we have modified our environment to meet esthetic and recreational demands. However, in solving some environmental problems, pesticides have created others of undetermined magnitude. The unintended consequences of the long-term use of certain pesticides have been injury or death to some life forms. Much of the information on the effects of pesticides comes from the study of birds, fish, and the marine invertebrates, such as crabs, shrimps, and scallops. It is clear that different species respond in different ways to the same concentration of a pesticide. Reproduction is inhibited in some and not in others. Eggs of some birds become thin and break, while others do not.

A Modern Dilemma

Residues of some persistent pesticides apparently are "biologically concentrated." This means that they may become more concentrated in organisms higher up in a food chain. When this happens in an aquatic environment, animals that are at the top of the chain, usually fish-eating birds, may consume enough to suffer reproductive failure or other serious damage. Research has shown that some pesticides decompose completely into harmless substances fairly soon after they are exposed to air, water, sunlight, high temperature, or bacteria. Many others also may do so, but scientific confirmation of that fact is not yet available. When residues remain in or on plants or in soil or water, they usually are in very small amounts (a few parts per million or less). However, even such small amounts of some pesticides, or their breakdown products, which also may be harmful, sometimes persist for a long time.

Pesticides, like automobiles, can create environmental problems, but in today's world it is difficult to get along without them. Those concerned about pesticides and pest control face a dilemma. On the one hand, modern techniques of food production and control of disease-carrying insects requires pesticides; on the other hand, many pesticides can be a hazard to living things other than pests, sometimes including people.

No clear evidence exists on the long-term effects on humans of the accumulation of pesticides through the food chain, but the problem has been relatively unstudied. Limited studies with human volunteers have shown that persistent pesticides, at the normal levels found in human tissues at the present time, are not associated with any disease. However, further research is required before results are conclusive about present effects, and little information exists about the longer-term effects. Meanwhile, decisions must be made on the basis of extrapolation from results on experimental animals. Extrapolation is always risky, and the judgments on the chronic effects of pesticides on people are highly controversial.

No Adverse Effect

Public concern about the possible dangers of pesticides has manifested legal actions initiated by conservation groups. Pesticides, like virtually every chemical, may have physiological effects on other organisms living in the environment, including people. The majority of the established pesticides have no adverse effect on people, animals, or the environment in general as long as they are used only in the amounts sufficient to control pest organisms. Pest control is never a simple matter of applying a pesticide that removes only the pest species. For one thing, the pest population is seldom completely or permanently eliminated. Almost always there are at least a few survivors to re-create the problem later. Also, the pesticide often affects other living things besides the target species and may contaminate the environment.

There have been and continue to be unfortunate and generally inexcusable accidents where workers become grossly exposed due to improper and inadequate industrial hygiene or carelessness in handling and use. Children sometimes eat, touch, or inhale improperly stored pesticides. Consumers have been inadvertently poisoned by pesticides spilled carelessly in the transportation of pesticides in conjunction with food products. These cases are, however, no indictment of the pesticide itself or the methods employed to establish its efficacy and safety. They are solely due to the irresponsibility of the user.

Pesticides are very rarely used in the form of a pure or technically pure compound, but rather are formulated to make them easy to apply. Formulations may be in the form of dust or granules, which usually contain 5% to 10% of active ingredients, or wettable powders or emulsifiable concentrates, which usually contain 40% to 80% active ingredients. It is important to remember that the formulations that are used as sprays are further diluted with water, oil, or other solvents to concentrations of usually only 1% or less before application. The amount of active ingredient, therefore, that is eventually released to the environment is generally extremely small.

Few responsible people today fail to recognize the need for pesticides and the importance of striving to live with them. Several national scientific committees in recent years have stressed the need for pesticides now and in the foreseeable future. These same committees also recommended more responsible use and further investigation into long-term side effects on the environment. It is generally agreed among scientists that there is little, if any, chance that chemical pesticides can be abandoned until such time as alternative control measures are perfected. . . .

Fear and Misunderstanding

The general public, most of whom are far removed from daily food production, have a poor understanding of pesticides. This is partly due to lack of understanding of chemical uses and agricultural production practices, but it is also due to fear and misunderstanding brought about through publicity of accidents and misuses involving pesticides. The perception of widespread hazards associated with presumed long-term accumulations of pesticides in people, other organisms, or the environment often appears to stem from lack of knowledge of the processes of metabolism, elimination, and degradation that largely preclude such perceived problems. . . .

Motor vehicles of all kinds kill approximately 50,000 people annually; 3000 die while swimming and 1000 people die annually in bicycle accidents. Approximately 30 people die each year from pesticides, which includes the tragic accidental ingestions mostly by children.

Individuals using pesticides and those concerned about pesticide use must seek all the facts and become better informed about the benefits as well as the risks of using these technological tools.

CHAPTER

3

AZT Is Not an Effective AIDS Treatment

by John Lauritsen

In the following viewpoint, John Lauritsen argues that the drug AZT should not be used as a treatment for AIDS. Lauritsen, a journalist, maintains that scientists have manipulated information about AZT to make it appear to be an effective treatment and have discounted information on its toxicity. Lauritsen believes AZT is a deadly chemical that harms AIDS patients. For this reason, he contends that treatment with AZT should stop.

As you read, consider the following questions:

1. How did the scientists studying AZT manipulate their research to make it appear effective as a treatment for AIDS, according to the author?
2. Why does Lauritsen argue that AZT is an ineffective treatment for AIDS?
3. Rather than using AZT, what course of treatment does Lauritsen recommend?

Tens of thousands of people are now taking a deadly drug which was approved by the United States government on the basis of fraudulent research. That drug is AZT, also known as Retrovir and zidovudine. It is the only federally approved drug for the treatment of "AIDS" (a poorly defined construct now encompassing more than two dozen old diseases).

AZT is not cheap. Treatment for a single patient costs between $8,000 and $12,000 per year, most of which is paid for, directly or indirectly, by taxpayer money.

The Most Toxic Drug

The most toxic drug ever approved or even considered for long-term use, AZT is now being indiscriminately prescribed on a mass scale. Even the British manufacturer, Burroughs Wellcome, doesn't know for sure how many people are on AZT, but it may be as many as 50,000 worldwide. The great majority are gay men, but the drug is also being given to intravenous drug users, hemophiliacs and other people with "AIDS" (PWAs). Children, including newborn infants, are now receiving AZT, as are pregnant women who are "HIV-positive" (that is, who have antibodies to human immunodeficiency virus [HIV], which the world-renowned molecular biologist Peter H. Duesberg has described as a harmless and "profoundly conventional" retrovirus). AZT is being given to healthy HIV-positive individuals, under the pretense that doing so will prevent "progression to AIDS." Some members of the "AIDS establishment," like William Haseltine (of the Harvard School of Public Health), have gone so far as to advocate giving AZT to perfectly healthy, HIV-*negative* members of "high risk groups," such as gay men, to prevent them from becoming "infected."

The prognosis cannot be good for these people. AZT's toxicities are so great that about 50% of PWAs cannot tolerate it at all, and must be taken off the drug in order to save their lives. AZT is cytotoxic, meaning that it kills healthy cells in the body. AZT destroys bone marrow, causing life-threatening anemia. AZT causes severe headaches, nausea, and muscular pain; it causes muscles to waste away; it damages the kidneys, liver, and nerves. AZT blocks DNA synthesis, the very life process itself—when DNA synthesis is blocked, new cells fail to develop, and the body inevitably begins to deteriorate.

The cumulative, long-term effects of AZT are unknown, since no one has taken the drug for more than three years. Even if patients were to survive the short-term toxicities of AZT, they would still face the prospect of cancer caused by the drug. According to the FDA [Food and Drug Administration] analyst who reviewed the AZT toxicology data—and who recommended that AZT *not* be approved for marketing—AZT "induces a positive response in the cell transformation assay" and is therefore "presumed to be a potential carcinogen."

Peter Duesberg has called AZT "pure poison." AIDS researcher and physician Joseph Sonnabend has stated that "AZT is incompatible with life."

What benefits does AZT have, that could offset such terrible toxicities? None, as a matter of fact. AZT's benefits tend to vanish as soon as one scrutinizes them. The oft-repeated claim that AZT "extends life" is based on research that fully deserves to be called *fraudulent*.

The belief in AZT's benefits appears to be based on three bodies of "evidence." First are the Phase II ("Double-Blind, Placebo-Controlled") trials of AZT, conducted by the Food and Drug Administration (FDA). Second are anecdotal reports. Third is a report which appeared in the *Journal of the American Medical Association* (*JAMA*). Let's look at these one at a time.

(This section is based on documents that the FDA was forced to release under the Freedom of Information Act. A detailed analysis appears in my article, "AZT On Trial." Whitewashed reports on the Phase II trials can be found in two articles by Margaret Fischl and Douglas Richman in the *New England Journal of Medicine*.)

Phase I trials determined that it was possible to give AZT to human beings, although there was never any doubt that the drug was extremely toxic. The next step was the Phase II trials, conducted by the FDA at 12 medical centers throughout the United States, beginning in the spring of 1986. This "double-blind, placebo-controlled" study was designed so that two groups of "AIDS" patients would be "treated" for 24 weeks, one group receiving AZT and the other receiving a placebo. Neither the patients nor the doctors were supposed to know who was getting what.

In practice, the study became unblinded almost immediately. Some patients discovered a difference in taste between the AZT and the placebo capsules. Other patients took their capsules to chemists, who analyzed them. Doctors found out which patients were receiving AZT from very obvious differences in blood profiles. Thus, the very design of the study was violated. For this reason alone the Phase II trials were invalid.

There are good reasons why blind studies are required for the approval of a new drug. The potential biases are so great, for both patient and doctor, that a drug-identified trial would be scientifically useless. Patients who believed that death was imminent without the intervention of a new "wonder drug" must have been psychologically devastated to learn that they were only receiving a placebo. Physicians, with high expectations for AZT, may have been biased not only in the ways they interpreted and recorded data, but also in the way they treated their patients. It is noteworthy that the public has never been informed by the FDA investigators, by Burroughs Wellcome, or by Fischl and Richman that the study became unblinded. . . .

AZT Was No Miracle Drug

When the Phase II trials were over, most of the patients decided to begin or continue taking AZT. At this point the miracle was over. AZT didn't prevent them from dying. In 21 weeks 10% of the patients on AZT died (whereas allegedly less than 1% of the AZT patients had died during the miraculous 17-week treatment of the Phase II trials).

Another comparison: After the Phase II trials ended, AZT became available on a "compassionate plea" basis, and survival statistics were kept on 4,805 "AIDS" patients who took AZT. According to David Barry, Vice President in charge of research at Burroughs Wellcome, somewhere between 8% and 12% of the 4,805 "AIDS' patients treated with AZT died during four months (= 17 weeks) of treatment. In comparing the two groups—each consisting of "AIDS" patients treated with AZT for 17 weeks—we find an enormous difference: less than 1% died during the Phase II trials versus 8-12% (call it 10%) following release of the drug. (See table.) A difference of this magnitude cannot be due to chance—the most likely explanation is that the less reliable figure (1%, from the Phase II trials) is wrong.

There are still more reasons for being skeptical of the mortality data from the Phase II trials. The theory behind AZT is wrong: HIV (as argued persuasively by Duesberg and others) is not the cause of "AIDS." And even if it were, a drug like AZT, designed to prevent the virus from replicating by stopping viral DNA synthesis, would be useless, since in "AIDS" patients HIV is consistently latent and therefore no longer making DNA. On top of that, there is no evidence that AZT has any antiviral effect against HIV in the body, as opposed to the test tube. (For a while pro-AZT researchers were claiming results from the "P-24 antigen test," an unvalidated and highly inaccurate test, but such claims have been abandoned."

Mortality Comparisons
(AIDS Patients Treated with AZT)

	Phase II Trials	Following Release of Drug
Bases: Total Patients Treated with AZT in Each Trial	(145)	(4,805)
Deaths in 17 weeks	1%	10%*

*The probability is less than one in a million that the difference (1% vs. 10%) could be due to chance. This powerfully implies that the less reliable figure (1%) is wrong.

Still further grounds for skepticism concern the ethics and competence of the researchers. People who would knowingly tolerate cheating, who would use false data, and who would cover up the unblinding of a "double-blind" study, would be capable of other kinds of malfeasance. There are many unanswered questions on how Burroughs Wellcome received exclusive rights to AZT, and how this terribly toxic drug gained government approval faster than any drug in the FDA's history. The National Gay Rights Advocates (NGRA) has charged "illegal and improper collusion" between Burroughs Wellcome and two federal agencies, the National Institutes of Health (NIH) and the FDA. Shortly after Burroughs Wellcome sent a check for $55,000 to Samuel Broder of the National Cancer Institute (part of the NIH), Burroughs Wellcome received exclusive rights to market AZT, even though AZT had been in existence for 20 years and Burroughs Wellcome had played no part in the drug's development.

Finally, the Phase II mortality data are suspect because the researchers performed no autopsies on the patients who died, and released almost no information on the causes of death. The FDA refuses even to divulge what cities the patients died in.

Summing up: It is highly unlikely that AZT extended the lives of patients in the Phase II trials. There are at least three explanations, not mutually exclusive, to account for the alleged mortality data. *One*, since the study became unblinded and the doctors knew which patients were receiving each treatment, the AZT patients, unconsciously or deliberately, may have received better patient management; the placebo patients may have been killed off through neglect. *Two*, the sicker patients may have been placed in the placebo group to begin with. (The FDA documents indicate that this was indeed the case.) *Three*, there may have been deliberate cheating: Some dead AZT patients may have been posthumously reassigned to the placebo group. Given the sloppiness of the trials, and the deplorable standards of the researchers, the third explanation is entirely plausible.

Aside from the doubtful mortality data, there is the issue of AZT's toxicities. The FDA analyst who reviewed the pharmacology data, Harvey I. Chernov, recommended that AZT should *not* be approved. Chernov documented many serious side effects of AZT, and summarized its effect on the blood as follows: "Thus, although the dose varied, anemia was noted in all species (including man) in which the drug has been tested.". . .

A Philosophy for Recovery

To be honest, at this point we do not know exactly what "AIDS" is, or what causes it, or how to treat it (although physicians are getting better at treating the various opportunistic infections). From all of the evidence, it appears unlikely that "AIDS" is a single disease entity caused by a novel infectious agent, HIV or other. Rather, "AIDS" appears to be a condition or conditions which may arise from multiple causes. . . .

If "AIDS" is really a degenerative condition caused largely by toxins, both medical and "recreational," then what is an appropriate treatment? Not still another drug, but rather freedom from toxins. Long-term survivors, almost without exception, have avoided toxic chemotherapy (like AZT) and have opted for repairing their bodies through a more healthy lifestyle: exercise, good nutrition, rest and stress reduction, and avoidance of harmful substances (including cigarettes, alcohol, heroin, cocaine, MDA, quaaludes, barbiturates, Eve, Ecstasy, PCP, TCP, Special K, ethyl chloride, poppers, and all other "recreational drugs").

Human bodies are the product of millions of years of evolution, in a universe filled with microbes of all kinds; if allowed to, they know how to heal themselves. Recovery from "AIDS" will come from strengthening the body, not poisoning it.

Oriental Medicine Can Help Treat AIDS

by Heidi Ziolkowski

Author Heidi Ziolkowski is a journalism professor at California State University at Long Beach. In the following viewpoint, Ziolkowski contends that the limited AIDS treatments produced by the federal government and the pharmaceutical companies have been ineffective. As a result, she argues, many people with AIDS are experimenting with alternative treatments such as meditation, acupuncture, and herbal remedies. These treatments, Ziolkowski maintains, have proven to be effective in easing the symptoms of AIDS.

As you read, consider the following questions:

1. According to the author, why could alternative medicine succeed in treating AIDS where more conventional medicine does not?
2. What types of herbal treatment does the author suggest could treat AIDS?
3. How does acupuncture affect AIDS patients, according to Ziolkowski?

If AIDS were curable through Western medicine like syphilis is, if it were manageable like diabetes, if it were a disease of those who suffer in silence and make few demands on society for research and treatment, and if it received little media coverage, alternative practitioners most likely would be assuming a far less prominent role than they are. Because Western medicine has no "magic bullets" to fire at the AIDS virus, there is room in the arsenal for herbal remedies, acupuncture, and meditation. Because the one disease–one cure approach of conventional medicine cannot adequately account for a syndrome which is a constellation of many diseases and many symptoms, those who have contracted HIV have begun to seek healing elsewhere, with varying results. One system they are turning to is traditional Chinese medicine.

Chinese and Western Medicine

For AIDS, the Western and the Chinese systems both have much to offer. The former has identified the causal virus and is better at diagnosing HIV (the human immunodeficiency virus); the latter carries with it centuries of clinical experience treating symptom patterns rather than single diseases. That approach is particularly well suited to AIDS, which is a complex of many diseases and many symptoms, few of which are common to all patients.

Though a discussion of AIDS does not occur in the literature of traditional Chinese medicine (TCM), it corresponds to the TCM symptom patterns, or conformations, of *xu lao*, which in translation refers to a class of conditions characterized by fatigue, especially due to repetition or long duration of an activity. This pattern is cited in a text from the first century B.C.E. [Before the Christian Era] as a deficiency of "vital energies" and organ systems. As noted by researcher and TCM practitioner Qingcai Zhang, M.D., in *AIDS and Chinese Medicine*, from a conformational viewpoint, AIDS can be seen as a severe "deficiency" or malfunctioning of the spleen, lungs, and kidneys.

Six-year HIV-positive survivor Marc Bluestein is representative of a growing number of PWAs (persons with AIDS) who are disillusioned with the Western approach to their healing. Even their term of choice to describe themselves—PWAs—rather than "AIDS patients," "sufferers," or "victims" is an indication of their willingness to take active roles in their health and not be cast as helpless spectators in some medical drama of drugs and physical decline.

Bluestein, who runs a Palm Springs "buyers' club" which helps PWAs acquire alternative therapies, says that he has taken a number of herbal formulas over the years. "At one time," says Bluestein, "I didn't know anything about Chinese medicine. I was exposed to only the typical Western medical model, but the conventional AIDS programs at UCLA and USC had nothing to offer me."

A Treatable Disease

He is under the care of Chinese medicine practitioner Melissa Nagel of Rancho Mirage, California, who, like many of her colleagues, sees AIDS as a "manageable chronic viral illness, not a fatal disease." Nagel believes that AIDS eventually will be thought of as diabetes is now, something which, though degenerative over the long term and potentially life-threatening, is treatable and controllable.

"I don't see any reason why I won't survive this illness," Bluestein says. "To hell with statistics! With AIDS, you learn to trust yourself."

Bob Felt, publisher of Brookline, Massachusetts–based Paradigm Publications, which specializes in books on Oriental philosophy and healing practices, is less cavalier about the importance of "statistics" and takes a more cautious approach. A longtime computer analyst and programmer, he says, "More rigor goes into the design of a commercial invoice than has gone into what some practitioners have proposed for AIDS. The pharmaceutical companies will continue to rule the world unless acupuncturists and Oriental practitioners learn to report clinical experience properly. There are so-called subjective improvements that they have the resources to report responsibly. Being able to say that patients feel better, are keeping up with their lifestyles, staying out of hospitals, buying time—these are worthwhile goals. Sadly, I'm afraid they will be lost in the noise of unsupported reports and the medicine show of hasty, speculative cures.". . .

Where does one go to find traditional Chinese medical therapies for AIDS? Major cities, including New York, Los Angeles, Boston, New Orleans, Santa Fe, Austin, and San Francisco, all have acupuncturists and herbalists who are treating AIDS patients. In rural areas or smaller towns it may be more difficult to find alternative health care; AIDS activist organizations in urban centers can supply names and addresses of clinics and practitioners administering TCM therapies.

The more complex issue concerns the value of TCM and related treatments. By its very nature, TCM focuses on the subjective, yet those who ask for verification are demanding objectivity. This means scientific accuracy, precision, and repeatability, which, in turn, means generously funded research.

Subhuti Dharmananda, director of the Portland, Oregon–based Institute for Traditional Medicine, says that TCM is in a catch-22 position: critics demand scientific studies and hard data, yet they are unwilling to fund such efforts. "A well-controlled study needs money," Dharmananda says, "and nobody has stepped forth with enough to put together a well-controlled study."

Daniel Hoth, M.D., director of the AIDS division of the National Institute for Allergy and Infectious Diseases, the leading federal agency in AIDS research, said he knew of no work being done with any Chinese herbs by the institute. "Research is funded by applying for grants, and it is tough competition," Hoth says. Though applications by researchers other than those working at established Western medical schools and universities "would not be rejected out of hand," Hoth could not cite a single instance in which such an application had ever been approved.

"There's an overall bias that nothing good comes out of China—only out of Washington and big American cities," says Martin Delaney, co-founder and co-director of the San Francisco–based AIDS awareness and activism organization Project Inform.

Compound Q

One of the most promising treatments for HIV infection, however, had its origins in Chinese folk medicine, not in Western medical research centers. Trichosanthin, an extract of the Chinese herb *Trichosanthes kirilowii*, used for over two decades in China to induce abortion, has been available in this country since 1987 under the name GLQ223 (Compound Q) for laboratory, clinical, and self-administration studies. Delaney called Q "the most effective drug we've seen" at killing HIV-infected cells.

Unlike conventional AZT treatment for AIDS, proponents of trichosanthin say that it is cell-specific, killing only infected cells and leaving healthy cells unharmed. This is a major advantage, since the immune systems of HIV-infected persons are already severely damaged, and any additional damage can be life-threatening.

"I feel like there's a light at the end of the tunnel," says James Beale, an Oakland, California, PWA and AIDS activist who has used Q intravenously and has experimented with rectal and sublingual (under-the-tongue) administration. "Compound Q has put my situation on hold. I'm not getting any worse and I'm even getting a little better. I'm not ready to say it's solved the problem, but it's part of the solution."

Data released in May 1990 would seem to bolster Beale's optimism, since eight of sixty-two long-term Q-users have "graduated" from a San Francisco treatment program administered by Project Inform. In Delaney's words, "There's nothing in their blood work that suggests that anything is wrong with these people." They have been "invited" to go off all further treatment, "not because we think that they're cured," Delaney says, "but because we don't know what this means." The best way to find out is to determine how they do without treatment.

Compound Q, however, is no simple herbal tea. A highly purified and concentrated extract, it is akin to chemotherapy, and, as such, it can produce side effects ranging from fever and muscle aches to severe allergic reactions and even coma or death. Delaney cautions, "It's dangerous stuff. You can't fiddle with it at home in your kitchen."

Approximately 1,000 American PWAs have tried Compound Q or the Chinese product, trichosanthin. Compound Q is still in the test stages and will not receive approval by the U.S. Food and Drug Administration for several years, if indeed it ever does. At present it is legally available only to those participating in clinical studies, such as through community-based treatment programs in Miami, New York, San Francisco, and Los Angeles. Some PWAs have begun to self-administer the Chinese counterpart of Q after obtaining it through the "AIDS underground," which makes new and often controversial treatments available to those who do not have time to wait for FDA approval. Ingesting the raw herb *Trichosanthes kirilowii* in lieu of Q is not a viable option, however, since the active ingredient, trichosanthin, is not present in sufficient quantity in the unpurified form to have any effect on the AIDS virus.

Traditional Chinese Medicines

Broadly, traditional Chinese medicine strategies for treating HIV infection fall into the following categories: herbs to reduce the potency of the AIDS virus; herbs to rebuild the HIV-damaged immune system; herbs that treat specific AIDS-related opportunistic infections and malignancies; therapies, such as acupuncture, moxibustion, and gi gong breathing exercises, which relieve non-specific symptoms; and herbs that lessen the adverse side effects of Western medications, such as anemia caused by the use of AZT.

In cooperation with Misha Cohen of the San Francisco AIDS Alternative Healing Project, Qingcai Zhang of the Oriental Healing Arts Institute began, in March 1988, a six-month clinical trial of herbal therapy for AIDS patients. This work has continued in the Los Angeles area, especially at Integrated Health Services in Lakewood. Zhang has treated more than 150 PWAs with the thirty-eight herbal formulas he designed and modified according to Cohen's clinical observations.

Practitioners throughout the country are using these formulas in their practices with good results. New Orleans nutritionist and health advocate Orisia Haas treats seventy PWAs with Zhang's herbal formulas, consulting with him several times each week to adjust doses. "I'm getting wonderful results," Haas said. "Some of my patients are completely off medication and doing beautifully." In those patients who choose to remain on AZT, she said, "The herbs mitigate the [side] effects of the medication, as well as the disease process itself."

Zhang's selection of herbs was based in part on pharmacological work done at the Chinese University of Hong Kong and the University of California, Davis. Researchers found eleven Chinese herbs that inhibited HIV production in the test tube. Based on these findings, as well as on an extensive review of current and ancient herbal literature, Zhang designed three groups of formulas: those immune-enhancing formulas directed at the suppression of HIV; those formulas for nonspecific complaints, such as night sweats, low-grade fevers, lethargy, and weight loss; and those designed specifically for opportunistic diseases.

Much of Zhang's most dramatic success has been with the third category. Viral infections, such as herpes, Epstein-Barr virus, and cytomegalovirus, are common in PWAs, as are fungal infections such as candidiasis, myobacterial infections such as tuberculosis, and protozoal infections such as *Pneumocystis carinii* pneumonia. Such opportunistic diseases are rare, or at least not life-threatening, in healthy persons with intact immune systems. "It is the opportunistic diseases that kill people," Zhang says. "No one dies [just] because he has the [AIDS] virus."

Of Zhang's formulas, one of the most promising, and one of the most commonly used, consists of viola (*Viola yedoensis*), epimedium (*Epimedium grandiflorum*), licorice (*Glycyrrhiza uralensis*), coptis (*Coptis sinensis*), prunella (*Prunella vulgaris*), astragalus (*Astragalus membranaceus*), and cassia seed (*Cassia tora*). Of these herbs, the first three have exhibited inhibitory effects on HIV in laboratory studies. Specifically, Japanese researchers have found that glycyrrhizin, the active component of licorice, appears to prevent an HIV infection from progressing to the symptomatic stage. Astragalus is an immune-regulating herb used in China as a tonic, and coptis has proved effective against oral thrush, a common fungal infection in PWAs. . . .

Immune System Cells

The most frequently discussed of the laboratory tests is the T4-cell count, usually referred to as simply the T-cell count. The normal average reading for an HIV-negative person is around 1000. T-cells are immune system cells that become infected with HIV. A count of healthy T-cells for PWAs is analogous to the blood-sugar readings diabetics take to monitor their control. Both tests indicate the patient's condition at the time of the test but do not convey the patient's status over time. T-cell counts thus can be misleading, since the counts of anyone, HIV positive or not, can fluctuate, especially when the person is under stress, as is certainly the case with those who are HIV-infected. T-cell levels below 100 are usually seen in terminal stages of the disease, although Nagel says she has patients whose T-cell counts are zero but who are still able to work full time.

"Lab work regarding T-cells is depressing," says Brian McKenna, acupuncturist and co-founder of the Austin Immune Health Clinic in Austin, Texas. "I question T-cell profiles as markers of either sickness or health. It's far more important that patients develop a positive attitude toward their health than it is to document their health via a battery of lab tests."

McKenna and other acupuncturists point to the improved emotional well-being, increased energy levels, and long-term survival of their patients as signs of efficacy. McKenna, who has treated over 200 PWAs, 60 percent of them for a year and a half or longer, has fifteen patients under his care who have been HIV positive for eight to ten years.

Michael Smith, a psychiatrist who treats intravenous-drug users and AIDS patients with acupuncture at Lincoln Hospital in the Bronx, agrees with

McKenna that T-cell counts "are not terribly relevant."

"If lab markers were a definitive sign of a patient's health, I'd have buried half my patients by now," says Smith. "I cannot think of a single case of a clear and consistent correlation between T-cells going up and the patient's overall health.

"[Besides,] I'm working with a city-hospital budget. I can't afford to do regular lab tests. One could wish that certain lab markers would [signal] a degree of improvement . . . but the most important question is, Are they still alive?". . .

Ted Kaptchuk, perhaps best known for *The Web That Has No Weaver*, a book that has become a classic introduction to TCM, expresses some concerns. "Any intervention gives hope, and hope can bring about improvement," he says. "I'm just saying that I don't know if the improvement can be linked to the efficacy of the herbs or to the enthusiasm of the practitioner."

Kaptchuk directed an alternative healing project that treated, among others, AIDS patients, at Lemuel Shattuck Hospital in Jamaica Plain, Massachusetts, for several years, yet he remains skeptical of what Chinese medicine can specifically do for AIDS. Throughout history, he says, there have been "many major plagues, but what has been shown is that Chinese medicine is largely helpless when faced with pestilent diseases. What the practitioners found is that all the people died, regardless of whether they had 'yang or yin deficiencies.' . . . Anyone who says that Oriental medicine has an answer to AIDS is not taking notice of history."

CHAPTER

5

Censoring Obscene Music Is Justified

by John Leo

John Leo is a columnist for the weekly magazine *U.S. News & World Report.* In the following viewpoint, he argues that lyrics which degrade women should be banned. He maintains that rock music influences those who listen to it, which makes songs that glorify abusing women particularly dangerous. Therefore, he believes, First Amendment concerns about controlling offensive lyrics are outweighed by concerns for the well-being of women.

As you read, consider the following questions:

1. How has the reticence to quote lyrics influenced the debate over banning them, according to Leo?
2. Why does the author believe lyrics which demean women are dangerous to blacks in particular?
3. What evidence does the author cite to show that liberals are inconsistent on the issue of censorship?

The issue at the heart of the controversy over the rap group 2 Live Crew is not censorship, artistic freedom, sex or even obscene language. The real problem, I think, is this: Because of the cultural influence of one not very distinguished rap group, 10- and 12-year-old boys now walk down the street chanting about the joys of damaging a girl's vagina during sex.

Abusing Women

What we are discussing here is the wild popularity (almost 2 million records sold) of a group that sings about forcing anal sex on a girl and then forcing her to lick excrement. The squeamishness of the press about sharing this rather crucial information with readers may be understandable; the subject is obviously loathsome. But it has distorted the case, making the censors look worse and the rappers look better than they really are. This is not about "expletive laced" or "raw" or "bawdy" language that shocks the bluenoses among us. It is about the degradation of women, packaged and beamed to kids as entertainment, and how a free society that cares about its future should respond.

You would never know any of this, or understand the outrage, if you read the bulk of what passes for social analysis in this country. "The history of music is the story of innovative, even outrageous styles that interacted, adapted and became mainstream," *The New York Times* said in a safely abstract, headache-inducing editorial. (Taking the tolerant long view, the *Times* is telling us an old story: New cultural expression shocks us first, then enters the mainstream. Hmm. Does this mean that woman-abuse will become conventional and the *Times* doesn't mind?) The *Los Angeles Times*, scrambling for the same high ground, tells us that much rap "often deals explicitly with violence and sexuality" (though, alas, none of this explicitness could be shared with readers). The president of Manhattan's New School for Social Research says we are witnessing a collision between those comfortable with change and those yearning for a simpler era.

Missing the Mark

Most other commentary was even worse. Colleen Dewhurst imagined that all American artists were under assault. Tom Wicker saw the nation yielding to "the persisting fear of difference." Richard Cohen, normally a sharp analyst of the culture, took the what's-the-harm approach, arguing that flag burning and 2 Live Crew (routinely lumped together by many writers) were merely "bubbles on the surface of the culture." Juan Williams, in a brilliant piece in *The Washington Post*, showed a better grasp of what the harm is. He argued that in a society in which the black family is falling apart, young black males are particularly vulnerable to the fear and hatred of women being fanned by 2 Live Crew.

Hateful Music

Another black commentator, Prof. Henry Louis Gates of Duke University, made the case that black culture has many referent points and styles (including in this case, hyperbole and humor) that whites can't understand and should be slow to attack. A valid point, except that the most telling criticism of 2 Live Crew has come from blacks, who presumably have less trouble reading black culture. Stanley Crouch, the prominent critic and essayist, calls 2 Live Crew "spiritual cretins" and "slime." Crouch says that "sadistic, misogynist, hateful music" adds to the problematic attitudes already burdening the black middle class.

But the dominant opinion of the opinion industry, so far as I can see, is that no reaction is really called for: 2 Live Crew is, in Cohen's phrase, "yet another cultural day lily." Maybe so, but the group's misogyny does not take place in a vacuum. From Prince's pro-incest song to the pimp worship of some rap songs to Madonna's current ditty about how much girls like being tied up and spanked, some fashionably warped messages about women are pouring through the culture. Why are we so sure that tolerance of such attitudes has no consequences?

Attempting to argue that there is nothing new under the sun, some critics say that 2 Live Crew resembles Redd Foxx's scatological humor and is probably as harmless. But Foxx was talking to small audiences of adults. We are talking about a huge audience of young people in an era when the electronic media are hundreds of times more powerful than they were a generation ago. Much more is at stake. And since we are an entertainment society, venomous messages are more likely than ever to disguise themselves as harmless fun. Andrew Dice Clay's audiences seem to be mostly white, male, blue-collar and resentful. I admit they are not yet whistling the Horst Wessel song, but they bear watching.

This is an age in which many Americans are conflicted about censorship. Liberal opinion is firmly against all censorship, except when it comes to the restrictive speech codes recently embraced at certain liberal universities. (The only way 2 Live Crew could get in trouble with some commentators would be to enroll at Stanford and read their lyrics to a female student.)

A Red Herring

"Censorship is a red herring in this case," says Jewelle Taylor Gibbs, author of *Young, Black and Male in America: An Endangered Species*. "The real issue is values, the quality of life." Yes, indeed. Censorship is folly. So is standing around reciting the First Amendment as if that were the only issue.

The popular culture is worth paying attention to. It is the air we breathe, and 2 Live Crew is a pesky new pollutant. The opinion industry's advice is generally to buy a gas mask or stop breathing. ("If you don't like their album, don't buy it," one such genius wrote.) But by monitoring, complaining, boycotting, we might actually get the 2 Live Pollutants out of our air. Why should our daughters have to grow up in a culture in which musical advice on the domination and abuse of women is accepted as entertainment?

Censoring Obscene Music Is Not Justified

by Clarence Page

In the following viewpoint, Clarence Page argues against banning the sale of albums with lyrics which may be considered offensive. He also opposes arresting musical groups when they perform such lyrics. He contends that while some lyrics are sexist, there is no proof that they promote violence against women. Censoring rock lyrics, he writes, could lead to further censorship in other areas. Page is a columnist for *The Chicago Tribune*.

As you read, consider the following questions:

1. How has the controversy over 2 Live Crew's album actually benefited the group, according to Page?
2. Why does the author believe banning lyrics is an impractical way to fight sexism?
3. What future does Page foresee for censorship?

It is unfortunate that, as one astute civil libertarian once said, First Amendment cases often put you on the same side with people you would never invite to your home for dinner.

But those who want to curb the Bill of Rights are clever enough to single out the most objectionable and artless material they can find, hoping to pave the way to later assaults on the more commonplace and meritorious.

Today *Hustler*, tomorrow *Playboy*. Today Mapplethorpe, tomorrow *Time* magazine.

Today flag burning, tomorrow an essay that advocates flag burning.

The Controversy

That's how I find myself defending 2 Live Crew, a rap group that is growing quite wealthy enough without my help, thanks to the controversy surrounding its piece of work, an album called *As Nasty As They Wanna Be*.

A federal district judge in south Florida found the album to be obscene, a finding that helped sweep it from local record stores and led to the arrest of two band members after a performance in an adults-only club. Two days earlier, authorities also arrested a record store owner in Ft. Lauderdale who refused to stop selling the album.

The fuss has resulted in the album's becoming such a sellout success at record stores that I had a difficult time investigating the lyrics in question.

Fortunately, the Parents Music Resource Center, founded by Tipper Gore, wife of Sen. Al Gore Jr. and a tireless crusader against naughty rock lyrics, saved the day. The center offered to fax the lyrics to me, all nicely printed out like a Shakespearean sonnet.

I accepted the offer, although in hindsight I suppose a zealous prosecutor like Jack Thompson, the Florida attorney who spearheaded the drive to have 2 Live Crew declared obscene, could accuse us of conspiracy to transport indecent materials across state lines.

But it was worth the risk, just to examine the lyrics for myself and judge their merit, a right Jack Thompson seems intent on curtailing.

An Adult Audience

Here's my judgment: Thompson is right about the lyrics. They're filthy.

They're vulgar, awful, loathsome, odious, nasty, offensive, vile, putrid and disgusting. Oral and anal sex are described in graphic terms and women are treated as sexual playthings.

I wanted to wash my hands after reading these lyrics. But I don't find them to be a jailable offense.

To paraphrase Voltaire, I disapprove of what 2 Live Crew raps, but I will defend to the death the group's right to rap it.

I am less offended by the filthy lyrics than by the arrest of the band members. They were not distributing their music, if you want to call it that, to children. Nor were they performing in a day care center.

They were performing in an adults-only club. If people like the young, multi-racial crowd that attended the show in question want to spend their money on that, it should be their right, as long as they don't hurt anybody else.

Jack Thompson, who has represented abused women in the past, has convinced himself that filthy lyrics do hurt somebody else. He says he wants *As Nasty As They Wanna Be* banned because it might fall into the hands of children and he wants all performances of the lyrics banned because they glorify, in Thompson's view, the sexual brutalization of women.

Well, Thompson is right to call the album sexist. Its lyrics regard women as sexual playthings for the pleasures of men.

But if that makes it obscene, there would be a lot of books, videotapes, movies and, for that matter, television shows that would be banned, regardless of artistic merit, except perhaps for reruns of Lawrence Welk.

Like other censors in the past, Thompson argues without scientific evidence that a rise in dirty lyrics leads to a rise in rape and other violence against women. Actually, the rise in such reports is more likely caused by a growing awareness of the problem and a new willingness by victims to come forward and report their victimization.

Voicing the Problem

Unfortunately, Thompson has convinced himself that dirty lyrics are the cause of a social problem—sexism—when in reality they only are giving voice to the problem.

Once we begin to exempt from First Amendment protections words and ideas that offend some of us, the list of exceptions that affects all of us only grows longer. It does not shrink.

President Bush would outlaw flag burning.

Jesse Helms would outlaw homoerotic art.

Author and radical feminist Andrea Dworkin would censor any art, photos or films that, in her view, treat women as sex objects.

Some minority college students would censor all forms of expression that offend their sensibilities, including classroom discussions and student newspaper opinions.

Pretty soon, we wouldn't have much left to protect.

Who knows? Today 2 Live Crew. Tomorrow maybe this column.

CHAPTER

6

Media Violence Contributes to Society's Violence

by David S. Barry

The average American child will witness 100,000 acts of media violence by the end of elementary school, according to David S. Barry. In the following viewpoint, Barry argues that this increasing barrage of violent images viewed by young people since the 1950s has contributed to a dramatic rise in U.S. violent crime rates. To support his contention, Barry cites numerous studies conducted by the medical community that have proven a direct causal link between media violence and aggressive behavior. Barry is a journalist and a screenwriter.

As you read, consider the following questions:

1. According to Barry, what is the difference between media violence of the 1950s and that of the 1990s?
2. What type of television programming contains the most violence, according to the author?
3. Barry writes that many depictions of violence on television take place out of context and result in no consequences or judgments. Why do you think he makes this point?

If you were a teenager in the 1950s, you remember the shock effect of news headlines about the new specter of juvenile delinquency. The book *The Amboy Dukes* and the movies *Blackboard Jungle* and *Rebel Without a Cause* were deeply alarming in their portrayal of teenagers willing to defy their school teachers and beat up other students. The violence portrayed in those stories, terrifying as it was, consisted almost entirely of assaults with fists and weapons which left victims injured, but alive. It was nonlethal violence. The notion of American teenagers as killers was beyond the threshold of credibility.

Since the 1950s, America has [become] almost unrecognizable in terms of the level of criminal violence reported in everyday news stories. In looking for a root cause, one of the most obvious differences in the social and cultural fabric between postwar and prewar America is the massive and pervasive exposure of American youth to television. Behavioral scientists and medical researchers have been examining screen violence as a causative element in America's crime rate since the 1950s. Study after study has been published showing clear evidence of a link. And researchers say that the evidence continues to be ignored as the violence steadily worsens.

Grim Statistics

The statistics about children and screen violence—particularly that shown on television—are grim. You've probably seen figures that show an average of 28 hours of weekly TV watching by children from ages two to 11. For prime-time programming, which contains an average of five violent acts per hour, that works out to 100 acts of violence seen each week, 5,000 a year. But children also watch cartoons, which contain far more violence than adult programming. For Saturday morning cartoon shows, the violence rate spikes up to 25 acts per hour, the highest rate on TV. With children's programming added to the mix, the average child is likely to have watched 8,000 screen murders and more than 100,000 acts of violence by the end of elementary school. By the end of the teenage years, that figure will double.

Those numbers are not mere statistics. They do not occur in a social vacuum, but in a culture and society with a murder rate increasing six times faster than the population. Whether we like to acknowledge it or not, America is in the grip of an epidemic of violence so severe that homicide has become the second leading cause of death of all persons 15 to 24 years old (auto crashes are the first)—and the leading cause among African-American youth. In 1992, the U.S. Surgeon General cited violence as the leading cause of injury to women ages 15 to 44, and the U.S. Centers for Disease Control considers violence a leading public health issue, to be treated as an epidemic.

From the 1950s to the 1990s, America has gone from being one of the safest to one of the most violent countries on earth. Here are some numbers: In 1951, with a population of 150 million, federal crime reports showed a national total of 6,820 homicides, 16,800 rapes and 52,090 robberies. For 1980, with a population of 220 million (a 47 percent increase), the numbers were 23,000 murders, 78,920 rapes and 548,220 robberies.

In big cities, changes were more drastic. In Detroit, for instance, the 1953 murder total was 130, with 321 in New York and 82 in Los Angeles. Thirty years later, the Detroit murder tally was up to 726, the New York toll 1,665—and the Los Angeles murder total was 1,126. The fastest climbing sector of the rising crime rate is youth, with the past 10 years showing a 55 percent increase in the number of children under 18 arrested for murder. America now loses more adolescents to death by violence—especially gun violence—than to illness.

A Direct Causal Link

The reason these numbers belong in this discussion is that the medical community sees a direct link between screen violence and criminal behavior by viewers. In panel discussions on this subject, we usually hear claims from TV and movie industry spokespersons that opinion is divided in the medical community. Different conclusions can be drawn from different studies, so the arguments go, and no clear consensus exists. Yet, the American medical establishment is clear— in print—on the subject of just such a consensus. The American Medical Association, the National Institute of Mental Health, the U.S. Surgeon General's Office, the U.S. Centers for Disease Control and the American Psychological Association have concluded that study after study shows a direct causal link between screen violence and violent criminal behavior.

The research goes back decades. The 1968 National Commission on the Causes and Prevention of Violence cited screen violence as a major component of the problem. The 1972 *Surgeon General's Report on TV and Behavior* cited clear evidence of a causal link between televised violence and aggressive behavior by viewers. A 10-year followup to the Surgeon General's Report by the National Institute of Mental Health added far more data in support of the causal link. The NIMH report, a massive study covering an additional 10 years of research, was clear and unequivocal in stating: "The consensus among most of the research community is that violence on television does lead to aggressive behavior by children and teenagers who watch the programs."

A 1985 task force for the American Psychological Association Commission on Youth and Violence came to the same conclusion. A 1992 study for the APA Commission on Youth and Violence took the issue further, examining research evidence in light of its effects or implementation. The finding was that the research evidence is widely ignored. The APA report was authored by Edward Donnerstein, Ph.D., chair of the Department of Communications, University of California Santa Barbara, by Leonard Eron, Ph.D., University of Chicago, and Ron Slaby of the Education Development Center, Harvard University. Their 39-page report . . . states definitively that, contrary to arguments of people in the TV and motion picture industry, there is consistency and agreement in the conclusions drawn by the major medical organizations' studies of media violence.

After discussing a massive number of studies and an extensive body of research material, Donnerstein's study quotes from the 1982 NIMH report: "In magnitude, television violence is as strongly correlated with aggressive behavior as any other behavioral variable that has been measured."

Specifically, the report noted the agreement by the NIMH, the APA and the Centers for Disease Control that research data confirms that childhood watching of TV violence is directly related to criminally violent behavior later on.

Daily Assault

Adding scope to the APA report is a study conducted for the nonprofit Center for Media and Public Affairs in Washington, D.C. The CMPA tabulated all the violence encountered during an 18-hour broadcasting day (a Thursday) in Washington, including cable TV. The tally showed an overall average of 100 acts of violence per hour for a total of nearly 2,000 acts of violence in the 18-hour period. Most of the violence involved a gun, with murder making up one-tenth of the violent acts recorded. A breakdown by channel, or network, showed cable to be far more violent then network broadcasting. WTBS was clocked at 19 violent acts per hour, HBO at 15 per hour, USA at 14 and MTV, the youth-oriented music video channel, at 13 violent acts per hour.

The networks (except for CBS, whose violence content was skewed by the reality show *Top Cops*) were as low in violence content as PBS, which showed two violent acts per hour. ABC showed three violent acts per hour and NBC two. CBS, because of *Top Cops*, was tallied at 11 violent acts per hour. But only one-eighth of the violence occurred in adult-oriented TV entertainment. The bulk of the violence occurred in children's TV programming, with cartoons registering 25 violent incidents per hour—six times the rate of episodic TV drama. Toy commercials ranked with cartoons in violent content. Next were promos for TV shows and movies, which were four times as violent as episodic drama.

The most violent period of daily TV programming was mornings from 6 to 9 a.m. where 497 scenes of violence were recorded for an hourly rate of 165.7.

Next was the 2 p.m. to 5 p m. afternoon slot with 609 violent scenes, or 203 per hour. The morning and afternoon slots compared to 320 violent scenes in prime time, from 8 p.m. to 11 p.m., or 106 per hour, and a late-night rate (from 11 p.m. to 12 a.m.) of 114.

No Consequences

In addition to recording totals, the CMPA examined the context in which the screen violence occurred. The finding was that most TV violence was shown with no visible consequences, nor any critical judgment. A significant amount of the violence occurred in movie promos, where it was shown out of context. Music videos generally present violence without comment or judgment. Similarly, violence in cartoons and toy commercials usually occurs without consequences or comment. More than 75 percent of the violence tallied in the study (1,640 of the nearly 2,000 violent acts) was presented with no judgment as to its acceptability as behavior. Violence was judged criminal in fewer than one-tenth of the incidents. And, ironically, while violence in episodic TV drama and TV movies for adult viewers is subject to close scrutiny for context and suitability, the bulk of the screen violence viewed by children is not.

The studies mentioned above make a compelling argument, particularly when looked at as a group. But a study by Dr. Brandon Centerwall of the University of Washington Department of Epidemiology and Psychiatry takes the discussion much farther. In a study published in the June 1992 *Journal of the American Medical Association*, Centerwall looked for statistical connections between the change in violent crime rates following the introduction of TV in the United States.

Centerwall found this: murder rates in Canada and the U.S. increased almost 100 percent (92 percent in Canada, 93 percent in the U.S., corrected for population increase) between 1945 and 1970. In both countries, the ownership of TV sets increased in almost the same proportion as the homicide rate.

Centerwall's stark and unmistakable conclusion is this: white homicide rates in Canada, the U.S. and South Africa were stable or declining until the advent of television. Then, in the course of a generation, the murder rates doubled.

The APA study by Donnerstein, Slaby and Eron also makes the point that research evidence of TV violence effects has "for decades been actively ignored, denied, attacked and even misrepresented in presentations to the American public, and popular myths regarding the effects have been perpetuated." Consequently, Donnerstein says, a major education gap exists regarding television's contribution to the problem of violence in America.

Screen Violence Rises

The discouraging point made in both studies is that, despite the massive research evidence of screen violence as a direct contributing factor to America's homicide rate, the screen violence level continues to rise.

As a writer deeply committed to the constitutional guarantees against censorship, I don't like to hear the suggestion of government regulation of movies or TV. But it's time we at least face the evidence of what screen violence is doing to our children, and come to some sober conclusions about our responsibilities to the common good.

Media Violence Does Not Cause Societal Violence

by Mike Males

According to Mike Males, complaints about media violence are misdirected. In the following viewpoint, Males argues that research into the effects of media violence is unreliable and proves only a minimal relationship between media violence and real-life aggression. Males contends that the true causes of America's violence are its social problems, such as youth poverty, child abuse and neglect, and excessively harsh juvenile justice policies. Males believes that critics attack media violence because it allows them to ignore society's real problems. Males is a freelance writer.

As you read, consider the following questions:

1. Why do critics emphasize the effects of media violence on children and adolescents, according to Males? Does he believe that children are more strongly affected by media violence?
2. According to the author, what age group is responsible for the majority of crimes committed against young people?
3. Males enumerates three "embarrassing problems" with media violence research. What are they?

Forget about poverty, racism, child abuse, domestic violence, rape. America, from Michael Medved to *Mother Jones*, has discovered the real cause of our country's rising violence: television mayhem, Guns N' Roses, Ice-T and Freddy Krueger.

No need for family support policies, justice system reforms or grappling with such distressing issues as poverty and sexual violence against the young. Today's top social policy priorities, it seems, are TV lockout gizmos, voluntary restraint, program labeling and (since everyone agrees these strategies won't work) congressionally supervised censorship. Just when earnest national soul-searching over the epidemic violence of contemporary America seemed unavoidable, that traditional scapegoat—media depravity—is topping the ratings again. . . .

The campaign is particularly craven in its efforts to confine the debate to TV's effects on children and adolescents even though the research claims that adults are similarly affected. But no politician wants to tell voters they can't see *Terminator II* because it might incite grownups to mayhem. . . .

But the biggest question media-violence critics can't answer is the most fundamental one: is it the *cause*, or simply one of the many *symptoms*, of this unquestionably brutal age? The best evidence does not exonerate celluloid savagery (who could?) but shows that it is a small, derivative influence compared to the real-life violence, both domestic and official, that our children face growing up in '80s and '90s America. . . .

The Genuine Causes of Violence

When it comes to the genuine causes of youth violence, it's hard to dismiss the 51 percent increase in youth poverty since 1973, 1 million rapes and a like number of violently injurious offenses inflicted upon the young every year, a juvenile justice system bent on retribution against poor and minority youth, and the abysmal neglect of the needs of young families. The Carter-Reagan-Bush eras added 4 million youths to the poverty rolls. The last 20 years have brought a record decline in youth well-being.

Despite claims that media violence is the best-researched social phenomenon in history, social science indexes show many times more studies of the effects of rape, violence and poverty on the young. Unlike the indirect methods of most media studies (questionnaires, interviews, peer ratings and laboratory vignettes), child abuse research includes the records of real-life criminals and their backgrounds. Unlike the media studies, the findings of this avalanche of research are consistent: child poverty, abuse and neglect underlie every major social problem the nation faces.

And, unlike the small correlations or temporary laboratory effects found in media research, abuse-violence studies produce powerful results: "Eighty-four percent of prison inmates were abused as children," the research agency Childhelp USA reports in a 1993 summary of major findings. Separate studies by the Minnesota State Prison, the Massachusetts Correctional Institute and the Massachusetts Treatment Center for Sexually Dangerous Persons (to cite a few) find histories of childhood abuse and neglect in 60 to 90 percent of the violent inmates studied—including virtually all death row prisoners. The most conservative study, that by the National Institute of Justice, indicates that some half-million criminally violent offenses each year are the result of offenders being abused as children.

Two million American children are violently injured, sexually abused or neglected every year by adults whose age averages 32 years, according to the

Denver-based American Humane Association. One million children and teenagers are raped every year, according to the 1992 federally funded *Rape in America* study of 4,000 women, which has been roundly ignored by the same media outlets that never seem short of space to berate violent rap lyrics.

Sensational articles in *Mother Jones* ("Proof That TV Makes Kids Violent"), *Newsweek* ("The Importance of Being Nasty") and *U.S. News & World Report* ("Fighting TV Violence"} devoted pages to blaming music and media for violence—yet all three ignored this study of the rape of millions of America's children. CNN devoted less than a minute to the study; *Time* magazine gave it only three paragraphs.

In yet another relevant report, the California Department of Justice tabulated 1,600 murders in 1992 for which offenders' and victims' ages are known. It showed that half of all teenage murder victims, six out of seven children killed, and 80 percent of all adult murder victims were slain by adults over age 20, not by "kids." But don't expect any cover stories on "Poverty and Adult Violence: The Real Causes of Violent Youth," or "Grownups: Wild in the Homes." Politicians and pundits know who not to pick on.

An Excuse for Failed Policies

Ron Harris' powerful August 1993 series in the *Los Angeles Times*—one of the few exceptions to the media myopia on youth violence—details the history of a decade of legal barbarism against youth in the Reagan and Bush years—which juvenile justice experts now link to the late '80s juvenile crime explosion. The inflammatory, punishment-oriented attitudes of these years led to a 50 percent increase in the number of youths behind bars. Youth typically serve sentences 60 percent longer than adults convicted for the same crimes. Today, two-thirds of all incarcerated youth are black, Latino, or Native American, up from less than half before 1985.

Ten years of a costly "get tough" approach to deter youth violence concluded with the highest rate of crime in the nation's history. Teenage violence, which had been declining from 1970 through 1983, doubled from 1983 through 1991. It is not surprising that the defenders of these policies should be casting around for a handy excuse for this policy disaster. TV violence is perfect for their purposes.

This is the sort of escapism liberals should be exposing. But too many shrink from frankly declaring that today's mushrooming violence is the predictable consequence of two decades of assault, economic and judicial, against the young. Now, increasingly, they point at Jason, 2 Live Crew, and *Henry: Portrait of a Serial Killer.*

Dubious Research

The insistence by such liberal columnists as Ellen Goodman and Coleman McCarthy that the evidence linking media violence to youth violence is on a par with that linking smoking to lung cancer represents a fundamental misunderstanding of the difference between biological and psychological research. Psychology is not, despite its pretensions, a science. Research designs using human subjects are vulnerable to a bewildering array of confusing factors, many not even clear to researchers. The most serious (but by no means only) weakness is the tendency by even the most conscientious researchers to influence subjects to produce the desired results. Thus the findings of psychological studies must be swallowed with large grains of salt.

Consider a few embarrassing problems with media violence research. First, many studies (particularly those done under more realistic "field conditions") show no increase in violence following exposure to violent media. In fact, a significant number of studies show no effect, or even decreased aggression. Even media-violence critic L.R. Huesmann has written that depriving children of violent shows may actually increase their violence.

Second, the definitions of just what constitutes media "violence," let alone what kind produces aggression in viewers, are frustratingly vague. Respected researchers J. Singer and D. Singer found in a comprehensive 1986 study that "later aggressive behavior was predicted by earlier heavy viewing of public television's fast-paced *Sesame Street*." The Parent's Music Resource Center heartily endorsed the band U2 as "healthy and inspiring" for youth to listen to—yet U2's song "Pistol Weighing Heavy" was cited in psychiatric testimony as a key inspiration for the 1989 killing of actress Rebecca Schaeffer.

Third, if, as media critics claim, media violence is the, or even just a, prime cause of youth violence, we might expect to see similar rates of violence among all those exposed to similar amounts of violence in the media, regardless of race, gender, region, economic status, or other demographic differences. Yet this is far from the case.

Inconsistencies and Contradictions

Consider the issue of race. Surveys show that while black and white families have access to similar commercial television coverage, white families are much more likely to subscribe to violent cable channels. Yet murder arrests among black youth are 12 times higher than among white, non-Hispanic youth, and increasing rapidly. Are blacks genetically more susceptible to television violence than whites? Or could there be other reasons for this pattern—perhaps the 45 percent poverty rates and 60 percent unemployment rates among black teenagers?

And consider also the issue of gender. Girls watch as much violent TV as boys. Yet female adolescents show remarkably low and stable rates of violence. Over the last decade or so, murders by female teens (180 in 1983, 171 in 1991) stayed roughly the same, while murders by boys skyrocketed (1,476 in 1983, 3,435 in 1991). How do the media-blamers explain that?

Finally, consider the issue of locale. Kids see the same amount of violent TV all over, but many rural states show no increases in violence, while in Los Angeles, to take one example, homicide rates have skyrocketed.

The more media research claims are subjected to close scrutiny, the more their contradictions emerge. It can be shown that violent people do indeed patronize more violent media, just as it can be shown that urban gang members wear baggy clothes. But no one argues that baggy clothes cause violence. The coexistence of media and real-life violence suffers from a confusion of cause and effect: is an affinity for violent media the result of abuse, poverty and anger, or is it a prime cause of the more violent behaviors that just happen to accompany those social conditions? In a 1991 study of teenage boys who listen to violent music, the University of Chicago's Jeffrey Arnett argues that "[r]ather than being the cause of recklessness and despair among adolescents, heavy metal music is a reflection of these [behaviors]."

The clamor over TV violence might be harmless were it not for the fact that media and legislative attention are rare, irreplaceable resources. Every minute devoted to thrashing over issues like violence in the media is one lost to addressing the accumulating, critical social problems that are much more crucial contributors to violence in the real world. In this regard, the media-violence crusade offers distressing evidence of the profound decline of liberalism as America's social conscience, and the rising appeal (even among progressives} of simplistic Reaganesque answers to problems that Reaganism multiplied many times over.

Virtually alone among progressives, columnist Carl T. Rowan has expressed outrage over the misplaced energies of those who have embraced the media crusade and its "escapism from the truth about what makes children (and their parents and grandparents) so violent." Writes Rowan: "I'm appalled that liberal Democrats . . . are spreading the nonsensical notion that Americans will, to some meaningful degree, stop beating, raping and murdering each other if we just censor what is on the tube or big screen. . . . The politicians won't, or can't, deal with the real-life social problems that promote violence in America . . . so they try to make TV programs and movies the scapegoats! How pathetic!"

Without question, media-violence critics are genuinely concerned about today's pandemic violence. As such, it should alarm them greatly to see policy-makers and the public so preoccupied with an easy-to-castigate media culprit linked by their research to, at most, a small part of the nation's violence—while the urgent social problems devastating a generation continue to lack even a semblance of redress.

CHAPTER

Condemned to Wait:
A Book Review

by George P. Fletcher

George P. Fletcher is professor of law at Columbia University and author of *With Justice for Some: Victims' Rights in Criminal Trials*.

Nothing focuses a man's mind like the thought that he will hang in the morning. In the modern version of this paraphrased bon mot from Samuel Johnson, the story ends less predictably. Morning comes, but the hangman might not. The problem is not simply that the electric chair and other more modern devices, such as fatally loaded hypodermic needles, have replaced the gallows. The modern source of uncertainty is the legal system itself.

As philosophers have opined about the death penalty for murder throughout history, they seemed to have imagined a fast, flawless executioner hounding down the murderer and swiftly exacting justice. The impression you get from reading Immanuel Kant is that the processes of justice are automatic. The manslayer is linked with his victim, and the death of the latter entails the death of the former, almost as though there were no need for an intervening trial.

As David Von Drehle, an editor at the *Washington Post*, masterfully weaves the tale, however, we now see that "the intervening trial" has taken on a life of its own. The American public seems committed to the death penalty, and the judiciary appears to go along with this commitment. Yet anxiety about becoming the agent of an official killing has made judges super-cautious. There is need not only for a trial, but for automatic appeal to the state supreme court. In addition, the feeling persists that state executions are fraught with constitutional issues.

This implies innumerable ways to enlist the federal courts as barriers in the long march from homicide to execution. Because executions do not keep pace with convictions, the result is an unstoppable growth of the death row population.

Von Drehle draws a fine-grained, gripping portrait of the painful process of trying to put a convicted murderer to death. Though he covers only a 10-year period in the Florida courts, his study illuminates the mechanics of a machine that the American public demands but is loathe to examine under the hood. Supporters of the death penalty just want to see it happen. They certainly do not worry about the side effects. No one cares whether half the time of state supreme court justices is engaged by automatic death penalty appeals. Nor does anyone worry about the expense. At a time when cost-cutting is de riguer, we spend about three times as much on the process of executing a convicted murderer as it would take to keep him or her behind bars for life. For its avid supporters, the death penalty is something like war: You do what you have to do and worry about the bill later.

On the basis of intensive interviews with Florida's death row inmates, Von Drehle takes us inside the culture of the condemned seeking to live. Their techniques of psychological survival fascinate. They hoodwink correspondents, romance lawyers and refine their confined minds and bodies. On the verge of dying, they find sources of life. Their counterparts—the lawyers seeking to save them—find in their cause an inspiration and commitment that is the envy of every work-a-day member of the bar.

Von Drehle writes about these players in the drama of death with affectionate detail. The stories are so finely tuned that one has the feeling sometimes that the author must be making some of it up. After all, how can he know what a certain warden felt as he was pulling tight the straps on "Old Sparkie." Yet Von Drehle convinces the skeptical reader with an eye for odd detail—the brand name on a set of loudspeakers in the execution room—and his abundant documentation. He improvizes only insofar as the dozens of people he interviewed were playing with the facts.

Among the Lowest of the Dead generally avoids the victims' and surviving relatives' side of the story. He does include a loving portrait of one pair of surviving relatives, Dave and Wendy Nelson, only to make the point that survivors suffer added agony from a system that cannot reliably carry out its promise to take a life for a life.

Von Drehle never hides his opposition to the death penalty, but he does not argue for abolition either. His strategy seems to be that telling the story of the system's unpredictability should be enough to convince any civilized observer that we are wasting our time and money.

In the end, the reflective reader does not know whether Von Drehle's stories of the life impulse in the face of death prove that the legal system works or does not work. However you proceed, the death penalty seems inescapably arbitrary. If you execute all killers, you ignore relevant differences among offenders. If you try to assess these differences, you enormously complicate the procedure and, in the end, appear to be executing willy-nilly. Yet the remarkable fact is that despite the desire of conservative judges and politicians to root out the evil among us, their respect for legal procedures prevents them from doing so.

The Death Penalty Is an Effective Punishment

by Robert W. Lee

Robert W. Lee is a contributing editor to the conservative magazine *The New American* and the author of *The UN Conspiracy*. In the following viewpoint, Lee states that the death penalty is the only effective way to punish murderers and deter violent crime. He maintains that death sentences are handed down fairly and impartially, and that it is society's right and duty to protect the innocent and punish the guilty by means of the death penalty.

As you read, consider the following questions:

1. Why does the author believe it is impossible to accurately evaluate the death penalty's deterrent effect?
2. What factors does Lee blame for the expensive cost of death penalty prosecutions?
3. What comparison does the author make between self-defense and capital punishment?

A key issue in the debate over capital punishment is whether or not it is an effective deterrent to violent crime. In at least one important respect, it unquestionably is: It simply cannot be contested that a killer, once executed, is forever deterred from killing again. The deterrent effect on others, however, depends largely on how swiftly and surely the penalty is applied. Since capital punishment has not been used with any consistency over the years, it is virtually impossible to evaluate its deterrent effect accurately. Abolitionists claim that a lack of significant difference between the murder rates for states with and without capital punishment proves that the death penalty does not deter. But the states with the death penalty on their books have used it so little over the years as to preclude any meaningful comparison between states. Through July 18, 1990 there had been 134 executions since 1976. Only 14 states (less than 40 percent of those that authorize the death penalty) were involved. Any punishment, including death, will cease to be an effective deterrent if it is recognized as mostly bluff. Due to costly delays and endless appeals, the death penalty has been largely turned into a paper tiger by the same crowd that calls for its abolition on the grounds that it is not an effective deterrent!

People Fear Death

To allege that capital punishment, if imposed consistently and without undue delay, would not be a deterrent to crime is, in essence, to say that people are not afraid of dying. If so, as columnist Jenkin Lloyd Jones once observed, then warning signs reading "Slow Down," "Bridge Out," and "Danger—40,000 Volts" are futile relics of an age gone by when men feared death. To be sure, the death penalty could never become a 100-percent deterrent to heinous crime, because the fear of death varies among individuals. Some race automobiles, climb mountains, parachute jump, walk circus highwires, ride Brahma bulls in rodeos, and otherwise engage in endeavors that are more than normally hazardous. But, as author Bernard Cohen notes in his book *Law and Order*, "there are even more people who refrain from participating in these activities mainly because risking their lives is not to their taste."

Merit System

On occasion, circumstances *have* led to meaningful statistical evaluations of the death penalty's deterrent effect. In Utah, for instance, there have been three executions since the Supreme Court's 1976 ruling:

• Gary Gilmore faced a firing squad at the Utah State Prison on January 17, 1977. There had been 55 murders in the Beehive State during 1976 (4.5 per 100,000 population). During 1977, in the wake of the Gilmore execution, there were 44 murders (3.5 per 100,000), a 20 percent decrease.

• More than a decade later, on August 28, 1987, Pierre Dale Selby (one of the two infamous "hi-fi killers" who in 1974 forced five persons in an Ogden hi-fi shop to drink liquid drain cleaner, kicked a ballpoint pen into the ear of one, then killed three) was executed. During all of 1987, there were 54 murders (3.2 per 100,000). The count for January through August was 38 (a monthly average of 4.75). For September–December (in the aftermath of the Selby execution) there were 16 (4.0 per month, a nearly 16 percent decrease). For July and August there were six and seven murders, respectively. In September (the first month following Selby's demise) there were three.

• Arthur Gary Bishop, who sodomized and killed a number of young boys, was executed on June 10, 1988. For all of 1988 there were 47 murders (2.7 per 100,000, the fewest since 1977). During January–June, there were 26; for July–December (after the Bishop execution) the tally was 21 (a 19 percent difference). In the wake of all three Utah executions, there have been notable decreases in both the number and the rate of murders within the state. To be sure, there are other variables that could have influenced the results, but the figures are there and abolitionists to date have tended simply to ignore them.

Deterrence should never be considered the *primary* reason for administering the death penalty. It would be both immoral and unjust to punish one man merely as an example to others. The basic consideration should be: Is the punishment deserved? If not, it should not be administered regardless of what its deterrent impact might be. After all, once deterrence supersedes justice as the basis for a criminal sanction, the guilt or innocence of the accused becomes largely irrelevant. Deterrence can be achieved as effectively by executing an innocent person as a guilty one (something that communists and other totalitarians discovered long ago). If a punishment administered to one person deters someone else from committing a crime, fine. But that result should be viewed as a bonus of justice properly applied, not as a reason for the punishment. The decisive consideration should be: Has the accused *earned* the penalty?

The Cost of Execution

The exorbitant financial expense of death penalty cases is regularly cited by abolitionists as a reason for abolishing capital punishment altogether. They prefer to ignore, however, the extent to which they themselves are responsible for the interminable legal maneuvers that run up the costs.

A 1982 study by the abolitionist New York State Defenders Association—based on proposed (but never enacted) legislation to reinstate capital punishment in New York (Governor Mario Cuomo has vetoed death penalty legislation seven times in recent years)—speculated that a capital case involving only the first three levels of review (trial and penalty, appeal to the state Court of Appeals, and review by the U.S. Supreme Court) would cost $1.8 million per case, compared to the projected cost of imprisoning a felon for 40 years of $602,000. In another study, the *Miami Herald* calculated that it had cost Florida taxpayers $57.2 million to execute 18 men ($3.17 million each), whereas keeping a prisoner in jail for life (40 years) costs $515,996 ($12,899.91 per year). Abolitionists tend, we suspect, to exaggerate death-penalty costs while understating the expense of life imprisonment. According to the Justice Department, for instance, it costs around

$20,000 a year to house a prisoner ($1 million over 40 years). Other sources peg it as high as $25,000.

As presently pursued, death-penalty prosecutions *are* outrageously expensive. But, again, the cost is primarily due to redundant appeals, time-consuming delays, bizarre court rulings, and legal histrionics by defense attorneys:

• Willie Darden, who had already survived three death warrants, was scheduled to die in Florida's electric chair on September 4, 1985 for a murder he had committed in 1973. Darden's lawyer made a last-minute emergency appeal to the Supreme Court, which voted against postponing the execution until a formal appeal could be filed. So the attorney (in what he later described as "last-minute ingenuity") then requested that the emergency appeal be technically transformed into a formal appeal. Four Justices agreed (enough to force the full court to review the appeal) and the execution was stayed. After additional years of delay and expense, Darden was eventually put out of our misery on March 15, 1988. . . .

• On April 2, 1974 William Neal Moore shot and killed a man in Georgia. Following his arrest, he pleaded guilty to armed robbery and murder and was convicted and sentenced to death. On July 20, 1975 the Georgia Supreme Court denied his petition for review. On July 16, 1976 the U.S. Supreme Court denied his petition for review. On May 13, 1977 the Jefferson County Superior Court turned down a petition for a new sentencing hearing (the state Supreme Court affirmed the denial, and the U.S. Supreme Court again denied a review). On March 30, 1978 a Tattnall County Superior Court judge held a hearing on a petition alleging sundry grounds for a writ of *habeas corpus*, but declined on July 13, 1978 to issue a writ. On October 17, 1978 the state Supreme Court declined to review that ruling. Moore petitioned the U.S. District Court for Southern Georgia. After a delay of more than two years, a U.S. District Court judge granted the writ on April 29, 1981. After another two-year delay, the 11th U.S. Circuit Court of Appeals upheld the writ on June 23, 1983. On September 30, 1983 the Circuit Court reversed itself and ruled that the writ should be denied. On March 5, 1984 the Supreme Court rejected the case for the third time.

Moore's execution was set for May 24, 1984. On May 11, 1984 his attorneys filed a petition in Butts County Superior Court, but a writ was denied. The same petition was filed in the U.S. District Court for Georgia's Southern District on May 18th, but both a writ and a stay of execution were denied. Then, on May 23rd (the day before the scheduled execution) the 11th Circuit Court of Appeals granted a stay. On June 4, 1984 a three-judge panel of the Circuit Court voted to deny a writ. After another delay of more than three years, the Circuit Court voted 7 to 4 to override its three-judge panel and rule in Moore's favor. On April 18, 1988, the Supreme Court accepted the case. On April 17, 1989 it sent the case back to the 11th Circuit Court for review in light of new restrictions that the High Court had placed on *habeas corpus*. On September 28, 1989 the Circuit Court ruled 6 to 5 that Moore had abused the writ process. On December 18, 1989 Moore's attorneys again appealed to the Supreme Court.

Moore's case was described in detail in *Insight* magazine for February 12, 1990. By the end of 1989, his case had gone through 20 separate court reviews, involving some 118 state and federal judges. It had been to the Supreme Court and back four times. There had been a substantial turnover of his attorneys, creating an excuse for one team of lawyers to file a petition claiming that all of the prior attorneys had given ineffective representation. No wonder capital cases cost so much! . . .

Lifetime to Escape

Is life imprisonment an adequate substitute for the death penalty? Presently, according to the polls, approximately three-fourths of the American people favor capital punishment. But abolitionists try to discount that figure by claiming that support for the death penalty weakens when life imprisonment without the possibility of parole is offered as an alternative. (At other times, abolitionists argue that parole is imperative to give "lifers" some hope for the future and deter their violent acts in prison.)

Life imprisonment is a flawed alternative to the death penalty, if for no other reason than that so many "lifers" escape. Many innocent persons have died at the hands of men previously convicted and imprisoned for murder, supposedly for "life." The ways in which flaws in our justice system, combined with criminal ingenuity, have worked to allow "lifers" to escape include these recent examples: . . .

• Brothers Linwood and James Briley were executed in Virginia on October 12, 1984 and April 18, 1985, respectively. Linwood had murdered a disc jockey in 1979 during a crime spree. During the same spree, James raped and killed a woman (who was eight months pregnant) and killed her five-year-old son. On May 31, 1984 the Briley brothers organized and led an escape of five death-row inmates (the largest death-row breakout in U.S. history). They were at large for 19 days.

• On February 11, 1990 six convicts, including three murderers, escaped from their segregation cells in the maximum security Joliet Correctional Center in Illinois by cutting through bars on their cells, breaking a window, and crossing a fence. In what may be the understatement of the year, a prison spokesman told reporters: "Obviously, this is a breach of security."

Clearly, life sentences do not adequately protect society, whereas the death penalty properly applied does so with certainty.

Abolitionists often cite statistics indicating that capital punishment has been administered in a discriminatory manner, so that the poor, the black, the friendless, etc., have suffered a disproportionate share of executions. Even if true, such discrimination would not be a valid reason for abandoning the death penalty unless it could be shown that it was responsible for the execution of *innocent* persons (which it has not been, to date). Most attempts to pin the "discrimination" label on capital convictions are similar to one conducted at Stanford University a few years ago, which found that murderers of white people (whether white or black) are more likely to be punished with death than are killers of black people (whether white or black). But the study also concluded that blacks who murdered whites were somewhat *less* likely to receive death sentences than were whites who killed whites. . . .

Flagrant Discrimination

The most flagrant example of discrimination in the administration of the death penalty does not involve race, income, or social status, but gender. Women commit around 13 percent of the murders in America, yet, from 1930 to June 30, 1990, only 33 of the 3991 executions (less than 1 percent) involved women. Only one of the 134 persons executed since 1976 (through July 18, 1990) has been a woman (Velma Barfield in North Carolina on November 2, 1984). One state governor commuted the death sentence of a woman because "humanity does not apply to women the inexorable law that it does to men."

According to L. Kay Gillespie, professor of sociology at Weber State College in Utah, evidence indicates that women who cried during their trials had a better chance of getting away with murder and avoiding the death penalty. Perhaps the National Organization for Women can do something about this glaring example of sexist "inequality" and "injustice." In the meantime, we shall continue to support the death penalty despite the disproportionate number of men who have been required to pay a just penalty for their heinous crimes. . . .

In 1953 the renowned British jurist Lord Alfred Denning asserted: "Punishment is the way in which society expresses its denunciation of wrongdoing; and in order to maintain respect for law, it is essential that the punishment for grave crimes shall adequately reflect the revulsion felt by a great majority of citizens for them." Nineteen years later, U.S. Supreme Court Justice Potter Stewart noted (while nevertheless concurring in the Court's 1972 opinion that temporarily banned capital punishment) that the "instinct for retribution is part of the nature of man and channeling that instinct in the administration of criminal justice serves an important purpose in promoting the stability of a society governed by law. When people begin to believe that organized society is unwilling or unable to impose upon criminal offenders the punishment they 'deserve,' then there are sown the seeds of anarchy—of self-help, vigilante justice, and lynch law."

Protecting the Innocent

To protect the innocent and transfer the fear and burden of crime to the criminal element where it belongs, we must demand that capital punishment be imposed when justified and expanded to cover terrible crimes in addition to murder.

The Death Penalty Is Not an Effective Punishment

by Matthew L. Stephens

The death penalty is arbitrary, expensive, and does nothing to prevent murder, Matthew L. Stephens contends in the following viewpoint. Stephens argues that death sentences are disproportionately applied to defendants who are poor, mentally retarded, uneducated, or members of a minority. In addition, he states that the death penalty is impractical: it is costly and does not deter crime. Stephens is a chaplain at Lebanon Correctional Institute in Ohio and the chairman of the National Interreligious Task Force on Criminal Justice, a body of the National Council of Churches of Christ.

As you read, consider the following questions:

1. What evidence does the author give to substantiate his belief that the death penalty is racist?
2. Why has the prosecution of capital punishment cases become so expensive, according to Stephens?
3. Why doesn't the author believe the death penalty deters crime?

When we look at capital punishment as an instrument of the administration of justice, we must ask: 1) Is capital punishment evenly applied to all cases of murder? 2) Will those charged in a capital punishment case have both the best lawyers and defense available to them? 3) Is the cost of carrying out the death penalty worth the money spent to execute one person? and, 4) Is capital punishment a deterrent to murder? After all, the latter is ultimately the question our society must answer. If it works, we must carry it out; if it doesn't, it is a ghastly and irrevocable error.

Applying the Death Penalty

In the United States, we experience the tragedy of over 20,000 homicides each year. These statistics are constantly increasing due to the devastating effects of drugs, racism and poverty. Yet, we choose, as a society, only 200, (or 1 percent of all murderers) to receive the ultimate punishment of death. When one looks at the criteria for selecting this nominal fraction of all murderers, the real issues come to light. Who are these people? What is their economic and racial background? What are their legal resources and representation? What is their intellectual capacity?

The facts are clear. Those on death row are the poorest of the poor. They are disproportionately "people of color": African American (40.7 percent), Hispanic (5.72 percent), Native American (1.49 percent) and Asian (0.61 percent), as compared to European/Caucasian. This means approximately 50 percent of all death row inmates are people of color in a society in which all of these populations constitute significant minorities.

Additionally, it is estimated that over one-third of all death row inmates are mentally retarded (with IQ's [intelligence quotient] of less than 70), and that nearly half are functionally illiterate.

It is these poor and oppressed children of God who become the victims of our society's anger and need for revenge. The death penalty is clearly *not* equally applied under the law, or under the more significant mandate of moral, ethical and spiritual values of a nation founded on these principles.

In a society that champions human rights and individual dignity in all of our creeds, we are far behind the rest of the so-called "civilized" western world in showing compassion to the poor and oppressed of our country. There are only two countries that still engage the death penalty as justice: South Africa and the United States. In 1990 the South African government officially put a "hold" on death sentences and executions.

There is overwhelming evidence that race is the single most important factor in choosing those who will be sentenced to death. Of the more than 3,000 people executed since 1930, nearly half were people of color. Eighty-five percent of those executed since 1977, when new death penalty statutes were passed, were punished for crimes against white victims. This is true despite the fact that the homicide rate for people of color is roughly 50 percent higher than that of the majority community.

Take, for example, the state of Ohio where 342 people have been executed since 1884. Of this number, only one white man was executed for killing a black person. In 1989, there were 100 people on death row in Ohio: 51 black men, 45 white men and 4 black women. Ohio has not executed anyone since the state reinstituted the death penalty, but the first execution will probably take place soon. Keep in mind that the minimum age for death sentencing in Ohio is 18.

The Case of Willie Darden

Consider the historic case of Willie Jasper Darden, executed March 15, 1988 in Florida's electric chair. He was 54 years old. Willie Darden was sentenced to death for the murder of a furniture store owner in Lakeland, Florida. Darden proclaimed his innocence from the moment of his arrest until the moment of his execution, over 14 years later. Significant doubt of Darden's guilt remains.

Willie Darden was tried by an all-white jury in Inverness, Florida, a county with a history of racial segregation and oppression. The prosecutor's opening remarks in the trial demonstrate the racial implications of this case:

> . . . The testimony is going to show, I think very shortly, when the trial starts, that the victims in this case were white. And of course, Mr. Darden, the defendant, is black. Can each of you tell me you can try Mr. Darden as if he was white?

Throughout the trial, the prosecutor characterized Darden as subhuman, saying such things as, "Willie Darden is an animal who should be placed on a leash." The US Supreme Court sharply criticized this misconduct, but refused to find that it unfairly influenced the trial.

In the face of evidence that those who kill whites in Florida are nearly five times more likely to be sentenced to death than those who kill blacks, the prosecution of Willie Darden becomes the story of a man who may well have been innocent, but whose protestations were overshadowed by the color of his victim and himself.

Finally, consider the case of Delbert Tibbs who went from Chicago Theological Seminary to Florida's death row. Luckily, he did not "graduate" from either. Deciding to take some time off from his studies, he hitchhiked across country. "White boys could drop out to 'find themselves,'" says Tibbs, "but nobody ever heard of a black man needing to do the same thing." His journey ended abruptly when, being in the wrong place at the wrong time, he was arrested and later convicted for the rape of a 16-year-old girl and the murder of her boyfriend in 1974. He was sentenced to death.

It was only with the assistance of the National Council of Churches Defense Fund attorneys that on appeal, his conviction was overturned on the grounds that it was not supported by the weight of the evidence. However, he was never said to be innocent of the crime. In spite of a US Supreme Court decision that he could be retried, the state decided not to reopen the case on the grounds that the police investigation of the crime was tainted from the start. The original prosecutor said, "If there is a retrial, I will appear as a witness for Mr. Tibbs." Today, Delbert Tibbs devotes his life to his family and to anti-death penalty work across the nation and around the world.

Defending the Accused

It is more than clear that race is the single-most contributing factor to one being dealt the death penalty. In combination with poverty, lack of adequate legal representation and the drive of society for vengeance, people of color are the common victims of this catharsis of hate and cycle of violence.

The quality of legal representation of indigent defendants in capital cases is of widespread concern. Most capital defendants cannot afford to pay for their own counsel and are represented by court-appointed lawyers in private practice, or by public defenders. Many times they are given inexperienced counsel, ill-equipped to handle such cases and working with severely limited resources. Many public defenders' offices are overextended with caseloads and cannot devote the time necessary to defend a capital case.

In rural areas, lawyers handling capital cases have little or no experience in criminal law; many are ignorant of the special issues relating to capital punishment. A recent study found that capital defendants in Texas with court-appointed lawyers were more than twice as likely to receive death sentences than those who retained counsel. The trial lawyers of a number of executed prisoners were found to have spent very little time preparing the case for trial. Often, they failed to interview potentially important witnesses or to raise mitigating factors at the proper times.

A good example of this problem is the case of John Young, a black man executed in Georgia. He was convicted in 1976 of murdering three elderly people while under the influence of drugs. He was 18 years old. His trial lawyer was disbarred from legal practice within days after the trial and left the state of Georgia.

When the lawyer learned of the execution, he came forward and submitted an affidavit to the court in which he admitted spending hardly any time preparing for the case, due to personal problems. He admitted he did not investigate his client's background or raise any mitigating circumstances at the sentencing stage of the trial that might have influenced the jury's decision. These circumstances included the fact that at the age of three, John Young had seen his mother murdered while he was lying in bed with her. He later was placed with an alcoholic relative who turned him out on the street to survive at an early age. The US District Court and the Court of Appeals ruled that they could not consider the lawyer's affidavit as new evidence because it should have been presented earlier. John Young died because of inadequate defense counsel.

The Cost of Capital Punishment

Certainly there is the moral cost of taking a life, to make up for the taking of another life. There is no real way to replace one life with the death of another.

Yet when capital punishment is the choice of the courts, this is exactly what has been decided.

The moral issue here is: Do we have the right to kill, or is that the right of God only? This does not excuse one who takes the life of another. That is clearly wrong. They will have to answer to the vengeance of their God. We do have the right to demand restitution and protection in the form of taking away the freedom of that individual found guilty of taking a life.

Taking freedom from individuals who kill others has also been shown to be less costly than executing them through our court system. The current debate on side-stepping a lengthy appeal process is nothing more than a rationale to expedite the death sentence while saving money.

In 1972, the Supreme Court of the United States, in *Furman vs. Georgia* held that "arbitrary and capricious" application of capital punishment violated the Eighth Amendment prohibition against cruel and unusual punishment. This means that a defendant has to be prosecuted and convicted in a way that is extraordinarily righteous and free of any kind of prejudice.

This "super" due process requirement has made the prosecutions of capital cases enormously expensive. In a University of California at Davis Law Review article, Margaret Garey calculated that it costs a minimum of $500,000 to complete a capital case in California. It costs approximately $30,000 per year to house an inmate in the California system.

Between August of 1977 and December of 1985, only 10 percent (190 of 1,847 cases) resulted in the death sentence. Data from New York State suggests that if it adopted capital punishment, the cost would be $1,828,000 per capital trial. Assuming even a 0.75 percent failure rate, it would cost about $7.3 million to sentence one person to death in New York, compared with $4.5 million ($500,000 x 0.90 percent failure rate) to sentence one person to death in California.

Cost effectiveness is a weak argument when talking about the value of human life. However, even when put on such a shallow rationale as cost-analysis, the death penalty does not hold up.

It has cost the state of Florida $57 million to execute 18 men. It is estimated that this is six times the cost of life imprisonment. A report from the *Miami Herald* said that keeping a prisoner in jail for life would cost the state $515,964 based on a 40-year life span in prison. It would cost $3.17 million for each execution. The newspaper broke the cost of execution down to show $36,000 to $116,700 for trial and sentencing; $69,480 to $160,000 for mandatory state review, which is not required in non-capital trials; $274,820 to $1 million for additional appeals; $37,600 to $312,000 for jail costs, and $845,000 for the actual execution.

These figures should make us ask ourselves: Is the need for our vengeance worth all this money when the possibility that we still convict and execute the wrong person exists? What really guides our conscience—the money or the moral issue of state murder and street murder? Whatever side moves us, we must see that the cost of capital punishment is too high.

A Deterrent to Murder?

Since capital punishment has been reinstated as a legal sentence of the law, there is no proof that shows murder has declined in any of the states in which it is being used. In fact, some states show an increase in violent crimes.

People who favor the death penalty often believe it helps reduce the number of violent crimes. This may be true if the person who considers homicide would make a rational decision in anticipation of the consequences. This rarely happens because most homicides happen in the "heat of passion," anger and under the influence of drugs or alcohol.

Studies show that murder rates in states with capital punishment, such as Illinois, differ little from the states that do not have capital punishment, such as Michigan. In 1975, the year before Canada abolished the death penalty, the homicide rate was 3.09 per 100,000 persons. In 1986, that rate was down to 2.19 per 100,000 persons, the lowest in 15 years. In some states, the use of capital punishment increased the crime rate. In New York, between 1903 and 1963, executions were followed by a slight rise in the state's homicide rate.

A Need for Revenge

The recent cry for the death penalty in our country comes more from the need for revenge than for justice. The "get tough" attitude of the law enforcement community and our "kinder and gentler" government telling the nation that killing offenders will stop the rise of violence, is paradoxical. Could it be that violence begets violence? Could it be that as long as the state is killing, we are sending a message that killing is the way to solve problems?

With all of the various factors we have considered, it is clear, even to the casual observer, that the death penalty does not work. It cannot be taken back, and it is arbitrary in its application and racist in its result. People of faith must take a stand. We must choose the day when we will transform instead of kill, when we will "do justice and love mercy and walk humbly with our God" instead of perpetuating a system that is evil, barbaric, costly and ineffective.

CHAPTER

8

The United States Should Nationalize Health Care

by Steffie Woolhandler and David U. Himmelstein

In many industrialized nations, the government pays for the health care of all its citizens. In the following viewpoint, Steffie Woolhandler and David U. Himmelstein argue that the United States should adopt such a system of nationalized medicine. The authors believe that nationalizing America's health care would eliminate the need for private insurance companies, thereby saving money. This savings could then be spent on improving the health care of all Americans. Woolhandler and Himmelstein are physicians who teach at the Harvard Medical School in Cambridge, Massachusetts.

As you read, consider the following questions:

1. Why do the authors believe a cost-effectiveness approach to health care reform would be wasteful?
2. Woolhandler and Himmelstein provide some examples of how nationalized health care systems have benefited the British and the Canadians. Cite two of these examples for each system.
3. How would the authors address the problem of expensive malpractice litigation?

In a report issued in January 1993, the Commerce Department said that spending on health care in 1992 reached a record 14 percent of the nation's total economic output, and predicted that by 1994 health care costs for the nation would total more than $1 trillion.

In simple human terms, uncontrolled increases in health care costs have caused millions of Americans to forgo needed health care or to be bankrupted as a result of health emergencies. For federal and state budgets, the increases mean less money available for investment in education, infrastructure and other needs. For business, especially small business, the burden of health insurance has become increasingly difficult to bear.

At his December 1992 economic town hall meeting in Little Rock, Arkansas, President Clinton said that bringing down health care costs was a prerequisite to other essential economic reforms. But in his campaign, Clinton also said that he wanted to rely on market forces as much as possible, and he praised managed competition among insurers as a strategy to control costs. Managed competition, however, would leave existing industry structures intact and could attain savings only by limiting the volume of clinical services or the wage cost of health workers. Managed competition is unlikely to provide adequate health care coverage for those now uninsured or underinsured, or to effectively control costs.

As long as health care remains a commodity, in which access to care is based on ability to pay, the inefficiencies and administrative waste of the current system will prevent substantial improvement in coverage or reduction in costs. Aside from being inherently unjust, differential access to health care based on ability to pay requires the herculean administrative task of attributing each charge and payment to an individual patient. This compels health institutions to waste huge amounts of money on marketing and bureaucratic sieves that separate lucrative from unprofitable patients, services and procedures.

Need-Based Care

The abolition of billing for service would with a single stroke eliminate the need for the entire insurance industry and much of doctors' office and hospitals' administrative expenses. Distribution of funds based on health care needs, rather than market forces, would save the money now spent on marketing. Eliminating corporate profit from the sale of health care would free up money for expanded health services and research. And abandoning litigation in favor of no-fault compensation for medical errors could direct remuneration to victims rather than attorneys and insurance companies.

In contrast to these reforms, most mainstream health policy debate has concentrated on the optimal means of rationing care. Cost-effectiveness analysis is usually advocated as the way to minimize the ill effects of such rationing, but these analysts base their calculations on current costs, which include the sums wasted on bureaucracy, marketing, profits, high physicians' incomes and defensive medicine.

Based on the assumption that the health care system will remain essentially unchanged, the cost-effectiveness approach ignores the potential for saving through structural reform. Worse, the solution of rationing based on such analysis entails the collection of detailed financial data, additional administrative controls and further bureaucratic hypertrophy. In other words, additional administrative costs.

The extent of waste in our current health care system is much greater than most people realize. Conservatively, we estimate that 30 percent of health spending ($226 billion in 1991) is wasted on administration, profits, high physician incomes, marketing and defensive medicine, none of which goes to improve health care.

Everyone now acknowledges that health care costs are higher in the United States than in other industrialized nations. One of every seven dollars spent in the United States—14 percent of gross national product—goes to the health care industry. This compares to only 6 percent of gross national product for health care in Britain and 8 percent in Canada. And both those countries provide free care to all. Yet the advocates of managed competition claim that either a Canadian-style or a British-style universal health care system would be too expensive. Indeed, with the help of the media, they have created a popular perception that it would cost too much to provide uniform, free service to all Americans on the basis of need alone.

In fact, nationalization of the health care system would save both lives and money. A single-payer plan that eliminated the unnecessary costs outlined below would not only be less expensive than our present system, but would also save enough money to provide quality care for everyone. Left critics of U.S. health care, however, have focused on inequalities, arguing that universal free access would improve health care. Few have challenged the official ideology that the "free market" in health care engenders efficiency.

As a result, advocates of socialized medicine have not experienced the issue of skyrocketing costs as an opportunity, but as an obstacle. Yet the true obstacles to a national health service are not economic, but political and ideological. If the public understood the extent of waste in our current "free market" health care system, its days would be numbered.

High Costs, Poor Services

So let's look at the elements in the existing system that raise the cost of care without providing medical services.

First, administrative costs. Between 1970 and 1991, the number of health care administrators in the United States increased by 697 percent, while the total number of health care personnel increased by only 129 percent. Rapidly rising costs of health insurance overhead, hospital and nursing home administration and doctors' office overhead attest to the bureaucratization of medical care. In 1991 these costs totaled $159.1 billion, or 21 percent of all health care spending.

The 1,500 private U.S. health insurers took in $241.5 billion in premiums in 1991 and paid out $209.2 billion in benefits. The $32.3 billion in overhead paid for processing bills, marketing, building and furnishing insurance company offices, and profits for commercial insurers. In addition, the administrative costs of Medicare and other government programs totaled $10.3 billion.

Hospital administrative costs are more difficult to quantify because many personnel classified as clinical for accounting purposes do some administrative work. Internists in one academic department of medicine, for example, spend 18 percent of their time on administration, and social workers at many hospitals devote considerable effort to insurance reimbursement problems. But even excluding the administrative work of clinical personnel, vast amounts of money and human talent are expended on billing, marketing, cost accounting and institutional planning. In California, administration and accounting constitute 20.6 percent of hospital costs. Similar figures have been reported for hospitals in Florida and Texas. We estimate that, nationwide, hospital administration and accounting cost $57.6 billion in 1991.

In addition, nursing home administration accounted for 15.8 percent of total costs in California's long-term care facilities, and a similar proportion of Texas' nursing home costs. Using the California percentage projected onto the $59.1 billion spent nationally for nursing home care, we estimate administrative costs of $9.3 billion.

Finally, physicians incurred professional expenses of $66.8 billion in 1991, 45 percent of their gross income. Much of this is for administration. Secretarial and clerical staff make up 47 percent of non-physician personnel employed in doctors' offices. Much of their time is spent on tasks like patient and third-party billing.

These administrative costs have increased much more rapidly than overall health spending in recent years—16.4 percent compared to 10.3 percent for the most recent year for which we have figures. Costs of hospital administration have also risen much more rapidly than other hospital costs. At one major Northeastern teaching hospital, the proportion of total expenditures devoted to administration has doubled over the past 55 years. And so it goes across the board.

Simplified Billing

In contrast to all this, Canada's universal health insurance system, administered by the provincial governments, gives each hospital a single annual lump sum to cover operating expenses and pays doctors on a fee-for-service basis. Capital spending is tightly controlled, and binding fees are negotiated between the government and physicians. A Canadian hospital has virtually no billing department and little of the detailed internal accounting structure needed to attribute costs and charges to individual patients and physicians. Physician billing is simplified by the unified system, with overhead averaging only 0.9 percent of premium income, one-fourteenth of the U.S. private insurers' overhead.

In Canada, administration accounts for only 9 percent of hospital spending. Insurance overhead and hospital administration together consume 6 percent of total Canadian health resources.

In Britain, the National Health Service owns most hospitals, pays physicians on a salaried or capitation basis and has no insurance overhead. Administrative costs there amount to 5.7 percent of hospital expenses and central administration consumes 2.6 percent of total spending. Together these categories account for 6 percent of health spending, though recent market-oriented reforms may drive up these figures.

Comparing the Canadian and British systems to our own, we calculated the potential administrative savings in the U.S. would be $115.2 billion—15.2 percent of current health spending—using the Canadian system, and even more using the British system.

In addition to these potential administrative savings, separating corporate profit from health care could save substantial sums. Profits of health-related industries have soared in the past three decades. After-tax profits averaging 7.6 percent between 1978 and 1983 placed health care third among the 42 U.S. industry groups.

Profits represent health spending in excess of the costs of care, and there is no evidence to suggest that higher profits mean better care. Indeed, the scant empirical evidence comparing proprietary and not-for-profit hospitals and nursing homes supports the opposite conclusion.

Similarly, claims of greater efficiency in the for-profit health sector are not supported by current data. Private insurance plans have much higher overhead than do government insurance programs. For-profit hospitals economize on clinical personnel and services but have higher total per diem costs because of greater administrative and ancillary services.

Decreased Effectiveness

The pursuit of profit also diminishes the cost effectiveness of the health care system as a whole by basing resource allocation primarily on financial considerations. The profit-maximizing behavior of medical enterprises often conflicts with the cost-minimizing interests of society. Long-term cost-effective services that offer scant financial reward—immunization programs, prenatal care for the poor, nonpharmacologic treatment of borderline hypertension—remain underdeveloped. But vast resources are devoted to lucrative but unproven services such as executive stress tests, weight-loss clinics and coronary artery surgery.

Pharmacological firms also squander enormous sums promoting "me-too" formulations of popular drugs, while eschewing vaccines or "orphan" drugs for uncommon illnesses. Similarly, the option of home-based renal dialysis is unavailable in many areas, forcing all dialysis patients into institute-based treatment, which is twice as expensive (and more profitable).

Adopting the British model of nationalization or a Canadian-style tightly controlled public insurance system in the United States would largely eliminate the profits of health care providers ($2.8 billion in 1983) and financial institutions ($2.1 billion in 1983). Broader reform could curtail profits in drugs ($5.6 billion), medical equipment ($2.8 billion) and hospital construction ($200 million). Thus potential savings from eliminating health care profits range from $4.9 billion to $13.5 billion, depending on whether nationalization was limited to health providers or was extended to suppliers and construction as well.

Physicians' incomes make up another area of potential savings. In 1941, doctors in the U.S. earned 3.5 times as much as average workers. This ratio had climbed to 6.0 in 1990, when doctors' incomes averaged $164,300. We are unaware of any improvement in the quality of care as a result of this increase, and 70 percent of Americans now believe that doctors are overpaid. Further, current reimbursement mechanisms skew the distribution of physician services toward financial rather than health needs and have increased disparities between primary care providers and specialists.

The impact of a national health program on physician incomes would depend on the fee or salary scale. In 1982, the average Canadian doctor earned $97,000 (Canadian dollars), 4.8 times the average wage, and disparities among specialists were considerably smaller than in the United States. Inter-speciality inequalities are also smaller in Britain, where in 1980 the average physician earned 2.3 times the average male worker's wage. If U.S. doctors' incomes were reduced to the level found in Canada or England, savings of $20.4 or $44.9 billion would be achieved.

Saving Money on Drug Advertising

Drug marketing is yet another source of potential savings—to the tune of at least $4 billion now spent on advertising and "detailing." Some argue that such marketing is not only expensive, but that it also adversely affects physicians' prescribing habits. Similar arguments apply to advertising for medical equipment and supplies.

Advertising by hospitals, HIMOs and other health providers has increased dramatically in recent years. Hospital industry sources estimate that advertising and marketing account for 1 percent of total not-for-profit spending and between 3 and 5 percent of for-profit spending. Based on these figures, provider marketing costs at least $3.4 billion in 1991. Total marketing and advertising costs exceeded $7.4 billion in 1991. If reimbursement under a national health program excluded compensation for such activity, at least that much more could be saved.

And finally, we have the legal profession, which has become increasingly entangled in health care. The legal complexity of medical practice and administration now requires many hospitals to retain full-time legal counsel. Malpractice litigation and so-called defensive medicine (excessive diagnostic testing) consume considerable physician time and expense, with malpractice premiums alone costing $5 billion in 1983.

The effect of malpractice litigation on the quality of care is at best uncertain. Litigation is an inefficient and capricious way to assure quality care. Between 66 and 80 percent of malpractice premiums are consumed by legal costs and insurance overhead, yet while 8 percent of doctors are sued each year, fewer than 300 verdicts favor the patients. Even assuming that many cases are settled without trial, the financial benefits to patients are tiny compared with those to lawyers.

A national no-fault compensation system for iatrogenic damage or error, modeled on the Swedish malpractice system or New Zealand's accident compensation system, would compensate patients more fairly and reduce legal fees. Considerable savings would also result from the abolition of incentives for defensive medicine, estimated to cost about $15 billion annually. Based on the lower figure, and assuming that some of this potential saving has already been included in our calculation of administrative costs and profits, legal reform might yield savings of at least $15 billion.

In the light of all of the above inefficiencies and waste—amounting to some $138 billion by our most conservative estimates—it is striking that most health care "experts" see cost control and equality in health care as contradictory. We believe that any honest comparison of our current system to those of the countries closest to us in culture and history clearly shows the superiority of socialized medicine. We think that most Americans would prefer such a system to the preservation of a private system that protects profit and privilege while remaining blind to waste and want.

Index

Reprint Credits